Implementing Ecosystem-based Management Approaches in Canada's Forests

A SCIENCE-POLICY DIALOGUE

Edited by
Brenda McAfee and
Christian Malouin

Published by

Natural Resources Canada
Canadian Forest Service
Science and Programs Branch
Ottawa

Copies of this publication may be obtained free of charge from
Natural Resources Canada
Communications Branch
580 Booth Street, 12th Floor
Ottawa, ON K1A 0E4
Phone: 1-800-387-2000
Fax: 613-740-3114

A pdf version of this publication is available through the Canadian Forest Service's Bookstore:
http://bookstore.cfs.nrcan.gc.ca

Cet ouvrage est publié en français sous le titre : *Mise en œuvre de méthodes de gestion écosystémique dans les forêts du Canada : un dialogue entre sciences et politiques*

Editing: Catherine Carmody and Paula Irving
Design and layout: Sandra Bernier and Julie Piché

Photograph Credits

Cover: *Left and center,* Petawawa Research Forest collection; *Right,* John Nagy, Government of the Northwest Territories, Department of Environment and Natural Resources, Inuvik, NT. All aerial photographs are courtesy of the National Air Photo Library, Natural Resources Canada (NRCan). Pages 3, 13, 17, 33, 87, and 101, Jacques Robert, NRCan, Canadian Forest Service (CFS), Laurentian Forestry Centre, Québec, QC. Pages 5, 38, 42, 53, 57, 63, 78, and 95, *The Forests of Canada* collection (NRCan, CFS, 2003). Page 7, Reg Parsons, NRCan, CFS, Atlantic Forestry Centre, Corner Brook, NL. Page 23, courtesy of Fisheries and Oceans Canada. Pages 26, 49, and 71, courtesy of the Geological Survey of Canada, NRCan.

Library and Archives Canada Cataloguing in Publication

Implementing ecosystem-based management approaches in Canada's forests: A science-policy dialogue / edited by Brenda McAfee and Christian Malouin.

Issued also in French under title: Mise en œuvre de méthodes de gestion écosystémique dans les forêts du Canada : un dialogue entre sciences et politiques.

Based on material from the Science-Policy Dialogue Workshop (Sectors across Forested Landscapes: Sustainable Systems through Integration and Innovation), May 24–25, 2007, in Ottawa. Cf. Introd.

Includes bibliographical references.
Includes some text in French.

ISBN 978-0-662-48191-1
Cat. no. Fo4-21/2008E

1. Forest management—Canada.
2. Sustainable forestry—Canada.
3. Sustainable development—Canada—Management.
4. Natural resources—Canada—Management.
5. Biodiversity conservation—Canada.
I. McAfee, Brenda Jane, 1954–
II. Malouin, Christian
III. Canadian Forest Service. Science and Programs Branch.

SD414.C3I46 2008   333.75'160971   C2008-980096-6

Contents

Conclusions   87

Appendices

Contributors

W. L. (Vic) Adamowicz
Department of Rural Economy
515 General Services Building
University of Alberta
Edmonton, AB T6G 2H1
Vic.Adamowicz@ualberta.ca

Tony Andrews
Prospectors and Developers Association of Canada
34 King Street East
Suite 900
Toronto, ON M5C 2X8
aandrews@pdac.ca

Patrick Crist
NatureServe
4001 Discovery Drive
Suite 2110
Boulder, CO, USA 80303
Patrick_Crist@natureserve.org

Steve Curtis
NatureServe Canada
c/o Agriculture and Agri-Food Canada
K.W. Neatby Building, Room 2089
960 Carling Avenue
Ottawa, ON K1A 0C6
curtiss@agr.gc.ca

Andy Cutko
NatureServe
555 Browns Point Road
Bowdoinham, ME, USA 04008
Andy_Cutko@natureserve.org

Tom J. Fowler
Fisheries and Oceans Canada
200 Kent Street, Room 13s047
Ottawa, ON K1A 0E6
FowlerT@dfo-mpo.gc.ca

Steve Gordon
New Brunswick Department of Natural Resources
P.O. Box 6000
Fredericton, NB E3B 5H1
Steve.Gordon@gnb.ca

David R. Gray
Natural Resources Canada
Canadian Forest Service
P.O. Box 4000
Fredericton, NB E3B 5P7
David.Gray@nrcan.gc.ca

Ken Harris
Environment Canada
Place Vincent Massey, 3rd Floor
351 St. Joseph Blvd.
Gatineau, QC K1A 0H3
Ken.Harris@ec.gc.ca

Brian J. Hearn
Natural Resources Canada
Canadian Forest Service
P.O. Box 960
Corner Brook, NL A2H 6J3
Brian.Hearn@nrcan.gc.ca

Ole Hendrickson
Environment Canada
Place Vincent Massey, 9th Floor
351 St. Joseph Blvd.
Gatineau, QC K1A 0H3
Ole.Hendrickson@ec.gc.ca

Joan E. Luther
Natural Resources Canada
Canadian Forest Service
P.O. Box 960
Corner Brook, NL A2H 6J3
jluther@nrcan.gc.ca

Andy MacKinnon
British Columbia Ministry of Forests and Range
722 Johnson Street
Victoria, BC V8W 1N1
Andy.MacKinnon@gov.bc.ca

Christian Malouin
Natural Resources Canada
Canadian Forest Service
580 Booth Street, 12th Floor
Ottawa, ON K1A 0E4
Christian.Malouin@nrcan.gc.ca

Rongzhou Man
Ontario Forest Research Institute
Ontario Ministry of Natural Resources
1235 Queen Street East
Sault Ste. Marie, ON P6A 2E5
Rongzhou.Man@ontario.ca

Brenda McAfee
Natural Resources Canada
Canadian Forest Service
580 Booth Street, 12th Floor
Ottawa, ON K1A 0E4
bmcafee@nrcan.gc.ca

Peter Neily
Nova Scotia Department of Natural Resources
P.O. Box 68
Truro, NS B2N 5B8
pdneily@gov.ns.ca

Mike N. Patriquin
Natural Resources Canada
Canadian Forest Service
5320-122nd Street, 2nd Floor, Room 2066
Edmonton, AB T6H 3S5
Mike.Patriquin@nrcan.gc.ca

Jake Rice
Fisheries and Oceans Canada
200 Kent Street, Room 12s015
Ottawa, ON K1A 0E6
Jake.Rice@dfo-mpo.gc.ca

James A. Rice
Ontario Forest Research Institute
Ontario Ministry of Natural Resources
1235 Queen Street East
Sault Ste. Marie, ON P6A 2E5
Jim.Rice@ontario.ca

Morris Seiferling
Alberta Government
Sustainable Resource Development
Sustainable Resource and Environmental Management
9915-108 Street, 11th Floor, Petroleum Plaza
Edmonton, AB T5K 2G8
Morris.Seiferling@gov.ab.ca

Bruce Stewart
Nova Scotia Department of Natural Resources
P.O. Box 68
Truro, NS B2N 5B8
bjstewar@gov.ns.ca

Introduction

Governments have made commitments to balance environmental protection and economic and social development. Although holistic approaches for dealing with these commitments have been discussed for almost three decades, progress on implementation of integrated ecosystem-based approaches to managing development and conservation is at various stages of maturity across Canada. An array of initiatives put in place to test these approaches provides excellent case studies for shared learning and examples of how to overcome obstacles to implementation. This publication reports on the discussions at a Science-Policy Dialogue where participants from governments, industry, and non-governmental organizations shared their experiences with implementation of integrated solutions for managing natural resource and environmental issues. These discussions are supplemented with articles and case studies that can serve as a baseline for an assessment of the extent of progress on implementation of ecosystem-based approaches in Canada's forests.

A Vision for Implementing Sustainable Development

Discussions leading up to the first global United Nations Conference on the Human Environment in Stockholm in 1972 highlighted the need for a balance between economic development and conservation of the environment. A workshop organized by the International Council for Science stimulated the publication of *Adaptive Environmental Assessment and Management* (Holling 1978). It describes an adaptive approach to management based on an understanding of the structure and dynamics of ecosystems. In 1980, the Convention on the Conservation of Antarctic Marine Living Resources became the first international agreement to recognize the ecosystem approach. The ecosystem approach gained further recognition in 1992 when it was accepted as the underpinning for implementation of the Convention on Biological Diversity (CBD) and the other outcomes from the United Nations Conference on Environment

and Development in Rio de Janeiro. Examples of these outcomes include the Forest Principles—the Authoritative Statement of Principles for a Global Consensus on the Management, Conservation and Sustainable Development of all Types of Forests—and Agenda 21, the global action plan for sustainable development. The CBD defines the ecosystem approach as "a strategy for the integrated management of land, water and living resources that promotes conservation and sustainable use in an equitable way". Twelve underlying principles (the Malawi Principles—see Hendrickson, this publication) and five points for operational guidance have been developed to guide implementation.

Definitions and Applications of Complex Systems Theory

Sustainability links ecological and socioeconomic processes by recognizing the social benefits flowing from ecosystems. Understanding the nature and behavior of whole systems and managing human activities within the limitations of the systems are a means of integrating the two processes. Ecosystem-based management acknowledges the relationship between ecosystems and the people living in them. Management objectives focus on maintaining the system processes responsible for producing the resources not only on the benefits to be obtained. Attaining these objectives requires an understanding of the factors influencing resilience and the threshold points at which the system capacity for self-regulation is affected. Implementing an ecosystem-based approach to development and management will stimulate modifications in human and institutional behavior. Systems-based decision-making requires that the interests, values, and knowledge of all factors and all stakeholders are considered in defining the issues and the options for dealing with them. Managing uncertainty and the risk associated with decision-making in self-regulating complex systems requires integration of information across disciplines, temporal and spatial scales, and administrative boundaries.

In this publication, authors may refer to the ecosystem approach, ecosystem-based management, ecosystem management, systems management, integrated landscape management, integrated land, or watershed management. Even though there may be definitional differences among these processes, in the interest of promoting further development and implementation of holistic approaches to planning and managing human activities, all these processes are here considered as similar means for the same vision. This vision includes:

- Long-term sustainability of the ecosystem as the overarching management goal;

- Focus on broad, system-wide consideration;

- Focus on composition, structure, and functions of ecosystems;

- Integration of management objectives across multiple, temporal, and spatial scales;

- Commitment to adaptive management; and

- Dedication to collaborative management.

PUTTING THE THEORY INTO ACTION

In Canada, the first formal adoption of the term "ecosystem approach" was in the Great Lakes Water Quality Agreement in 1978. The ecosystem approach is clearly rooted in the *Canada National Parks Act* (2000) and the *Oceans Act* (1996). The *Species at Risk Act* (2002) also proposes an ecosystem approach to protecting threatened and endangered species. Reference to implementation of the ecosystem approach is embedded in the Canadian Biodiversity Strategy (CBS), the National Forest Strategy, and in several provincial and territorial biodiversity strategies, policies, and land management regulatory frameworks. In October 2006, the Canadian Councils of Resource Ministers and the Canadian Council of Ministers of the Environment approved the Biodiversity Outcomes Framework, an ecosystem approach to implementing the CBS. By agreeing to work together on this framework, ministers will ensure that biodiversity, resource management development, and the environment are considered from a strategic and integrated perspective.

In 2004, after much debate, a decision at the 7th Conference of the Parties of the CBD (COP7) acknowledged that sustainable forest management was a means to implement the ecosystem approach in the forest sector

but that further cross-sectoral integration was needed. This decision provided guidance for forest sector activities by recommending that sharing knowledge and expertise among practitioners and decision makers was a first step toward the integration of the ecosystem approach into land-use strategies.

Over 20 years ago, the forest sector moved from management focused on timber production to managing forest ecosystems for the multitude of benefits they provide. The Canadian Council of Forest Ministers' criteria and indicators of sustainable forest management provide a framework for integrating social, ecological, and economic aspects of management. This framework was the basis for the development of a marketplace tool to certify that forest products originate from forests that are managed sustainably. Canada's Model Forest Network, an association of in situ laboratories across the country, with links to the International Model Forest Network, has many lessons to share from its experiences in testing and implementing innovative, cooperative, cross-sectoral approaches to land-use planning.

Over the past decade, several workshops and studies have examined the implementation status of ecosystem-based management in Canada. A 1999 study of the trends in ecosystem-based management in federal, provincial, municipal, industry, and non-governmental organizations identified a willingness and a capacity to embrace ecosystem-based initiatives as an emerging approach in every jurisdiction across the country, particularly for natural resources and protected areas management and more broadly for sustainable development (Quinn and Theberge 2004). A 2002 survey of the ecosystem approach in the forest sector carried out by the *Institut québécois d'aménagement de la forêt feuillue* indicated that although there was general awareness and support, there was limited understanding of the concept and no consensus on implementation (Moreau et al. 2002.)

The mission of the Canadian Coalition for Integrated Landscape Management (formerly the Canadian Integrated Landscape Management Coalition) is to advance and accelerate integrated landscape management in Canada by influencing key decision makers in the development of appropriate policies, practices, and tools (see Andrews, this publication). The report from their 2005 workshop identifies an urgent need for expanding and accelerating implementation of the concept across

Canada (Canadian Integrated Landscape Management Coalition 2005). In the same year, a joint workshop was organized by the Policy Research Initiative and Environment Canada on integrated landscape management modeling to advance discussions on technical capacity. The workshop report describes how integrated landscape models can improve implementation of integrated management by focusing on gaps between policy, management, and research (Policy Research Initiative 2005).

The COP7 decision in 2004, referred to previously, encouraged Parties to continue to promote the application of the ecosystem approach in all sectors. The organization of workshops to bring together experts and practitioners from different sectors and approaches to share experiences and expertise was also recommended as a useful means to accelerate implementation. As preparation for the next review of progress on implementation of the ecosystem approach, which will take place at COP9 in May 2008, a Science-Policy Dialogue entitled "Sectors across Forested Landscapes: Sustainable Systems through Integration and Innovation," was held May 24–25, 2007, in Ottawa. The agenda and list of participants are available in Appendix 1.

OVERVIEW OF THE PUBLICATION

Much of the material for this publication originated from this Science-Policy Dialogue. The Directors' General Science-Policy Dialogues is a workshop and seminar series established in 2004 to promote integration of science and policy through shared dialogue. The Dialogues foster exchange of information and experiences to promote science-policy integration. The May 2007 Dialogue was a partnership between Environment Canada and Natural Resources Canada, two federal departments with a shared interest in improving integration of environmental protection and social and economic development activities. Participants from provinces and territories, federal government departments, and non-governmental organizations shared lessons learned from their experiences with ecosystem-based management approaches and identified solutions for common challenges.

The participants at the Science-Policy Dialogue recommended that the information discussed at the workshop be expanded and compiled to provide an overview of the status of implementation in Canada's forests. Assessing the current status of ecosystem-based management in Canada requires the establishment of an inventory of case studies and a comprehensive empirical evaluation of their strengths and weaknesses. Only a fraction of the jurisdictions, sectors, and organizations involved in ecosystem-based initiatives were able to attend. For the publication, we solicited information from as many additional sources as possible to provide an opportunity to those who were not able to participate in the workshop to tell their story. However, as a result of time constraints, this effort remains an illustrative sampling of the many types and approaches of ecosystem-based initiatives in Canada. We hope that this report and the array of case studies examined will provide a stimulus for continuing this Dialogue and lead to improved understanding and increased implementation of systems-based approaches to development and conservation across the country.

REFERENCES

Canadian Integrated Landscape Management Coalition. 2005. Integrated Landscape Management: Applying sustainable development to land use. 31 p. http://www.pdac.ca/pdac/advocacy/land-use/ilm-concept-paper.pdf [Accessed February 2008.]

Holling, C.S., ed. 1978. Adaptive environmental assessment and management. John Wiley and Sons Ltd., London. 377 p.

Moreau, A.; Sougavinski, S.; Doyon, F. 2002. Ecosystem-based forest management in Canada: Survey of projects and current situation. Institut québécois d'aménagement de la forêt feuillue. Unpublished report. 41 p.

Policy Research Initiative. 2005. Integrated Landscape Management Modelling Workshop Report, February 28–March 1, 2005, Ottawa, 25 p. www.policyresearch.gc.ca/doclib/ILMM_Workshop_Report_e.pdf [Accessed February 2008.]

Quinn, M.S.; Theberge, J.C. 2004. Ecosystem-based management in Canada: Trends from a national survey and relevance to protected areas in Making ecosystem-based management work: Connecting managers and researchers. Proceedings of the 5th International Conference on Science and Management of Protected Areas, Wolfville, Nova Scotia, 11–16 May, 2003. http://www.sampaa.org/PDF/ch8/8.2.pdf [Accessed February 2008.]

Conceptual
Thinking

Achieving Sustainable Development: Organizing to Focus on Systems

Ken Harris Manager, Landscape Science and Technology Division
Environment Canada, Gatineau, QC

INTRODUCTION

In this article, I provide an overview of how Canada's approach to natural resources management has evolved. I also discuss what Canada needs to change in its approach to managing the environment and how it can organize for such a change.

CANADIAN ENVIRONMENTAL MANAGEMENT: AN OVERVIEW

Environmental management in Canada began when people realized that valued goods and services of ecosystems were under threat from air and water pollution, water consumption, over-harvest of species, and other such forces. Environmental management often involved relatively simple linear responses to relatively straightforward problems. Some familiar examples are how the threats to specific species, such as the plains bison, various migratory birds, wolves, and beaver, from hunting, trapping, pollution, or loss of habitat, have been dealt with. Federal and provincial laws were conceived that banned or regulated harvest (such as the *Migratory Bird Convention Act* and the *Fisheries Act*), regulated pollution (such as the *Canadian Environmental Protection Act* and provincial water quality laws), and required environmental assessments (such as the *Canadian Environmental Assessment Act)*. The responses have been relatively effective because they too were relatively straightforward and focused on specific projects at specific sites.

The need to provide protection to places, features, and functions for the production of clean and abundant water and for the maintenance of biodiversity spurred the broadening of environmental management practices. This need has also been long reflected in legislation. In the 1800s, parks and sanctuaries were created not only to protect species from harvest but also to preserve significant wilderness areas for the public's enjoyment and to safeguard watersheds. For example, Algonquin Provincial Park was established in 1893 mainly to protect the headwaters of five major rivers. The [*Canada*] *National Parks Act*, dating back to 1930, the *Canada Wildlife Act* enacted in 1972 and, most recently, the *Oceans Act* of 1996 have established authority at the federal level to protect biologically or ecologically significant areas. In the last 40 years, various provinces have established watershed-based acts, programs, and/or structures to manage water on a systems basis.

Over time and with more experience in environmental management, researchers realized the limitations of approaches that focused only on specific products, sites, and features. These approaches were not designed to address interactions and interdependencies among ecosystem components nor consider ecosystem goods and services in the context of the health of a larger system. Despite Canada's investments in environmental management, ecosystem goods and services were declining. The nature of these declines lay not in decreasing outputs, excessive consumption, or contamination of goods and services, but rather in fundamental disruptions to ecosystem structures and processes. The science, data gathering, decision making, and programs that were effective for past approaches were inadequate because they were never designed to counter disruptions of a systemic nature. Of the hundreds of environmental laws, regulations, and programs across Canada, extremely few deal with system threats. Nor are they designed to be used in any coherent fashion with each other to counter such threats.

What Needs to Change

Currently, Canada has no forum nor process at the national level that would be a natural "home" for discussions or decision-making on risks and responses regarding the integrity of Canada's ecosystems—neither in general nor for specific ecosystems. Canada lacks a focused national effort on understanding ecosystem function and on predicting how ecosystems will react to changes. National and regional monitoring data sets have languished (for example, land cover mapping and species trends) and access to data remains a major barrier. Federal, provincial, and territorial governments and non-governmental organizations deliver their programming largely in isolation from each other, with little attention to common goals and priorities.

Why Canada Needs a New Approach

Canada needs a systems approach to systems' problems. Such an approach will help Canada

- understand the implications of its decisions and the nature of the trade-offs when responding to environmental threats;

- develop or select management tools that deal with the connected nature of ecosystems;

- consider ecosystem function at ecosystem scales; and

- include ecological, social, and economic aspects in management of its natural capital.

An Ecosystem Approach to Environmental Management

An ecosystem approach to environmental management concentrates understanding, decision-making, and actions on a whole system rather than its individual parts and their connections; it provides a systems context that recognizes limits to the degree of stress that systems can accommodate before they are irreversibly degraded. An ecosystem approach focuses on maintaining the capacity of a system to produce ecosystem goods and services by conserving ecosystem structures, processes, and interactions. More specifically, this approach

- manages human influences on ecosystems, not ecosystems per se, by understanding how these influences alter ecosystem function and outputs;

- considers ecological goals simultaneously with economic and social goals;

- takes into account trade-offs when making decisions;

- requires coherent and coordinated implementation of actions across the relevant social, economic, and environmental sectors, often within a defined geographic area;

- complements and enhances delivery of national programs by linking critical issues and integrating activities (such as research and monitoring) of national programs in targeted areas;

- makes national objectives (like the Convention on Biological Diversity targets, for instance) understandable to stakeholders and citizens at the "ground" level by providing measurable targets and clearly articulated results;

- extends the reach of national programs by strengthening partnerships with external stakeholders, leveraging resources, and enhancing relationships with key stakeholders;

- supports collective and integrated decision-making by providing

  - integrated information on the state of the ecosystem in a format intuitive to decision-makers;

  - a framework for engaging key stakeholders, be they landowners, industry, First Nations etc., and for fostering inter-jurisdictional cooperation in targeted areas; and

  - additional capacity in areas of the country where ecosystem threats are a priority;

- does not impose a geographic planning unit or scale—boundaries are set according to scientific, policy, and management assessments of the area or ecosystem under threat;

- is not about any single output (for example, species, water quality or quantity, clean air, stable and predictable climate)—it is a refocusing of management activities on the system that produces these desirable goods and services; and

- is not a program or a result—it is an overarching management approach, a shift in the way programs are conceptualized, designed, and delivered.

Making the Shift: Environment Canada's Ecosystem Approach Framework

In 2006, as a basis for internal and external discussions, Environment Canada staff undertook the task of designing an organizing framework for an ecosystem approach to environmental management. The proposed framework comprises the mandate, objective, and underlying principles of Environment Canada's proposed Ecosystem Approach to Environmental Management.

The Framework

Mandate

The Ecosystem Approach to Environmental Management focuses on understanding, making decisions, and taking action based on the long-term health of ecosystem structure, processes, and interactions and integrates environmental, economic, and social objectives within ecological scales and timeframes.

Objective

The Ecosystem Approach to Environmental Management aims to maintain a natural capital system that ensures a perpetual supply of the ecosystem goods and services that sustain the health, economic prosperity, and competitiveness of Canadians, while taking into account society's social, economic, and environmental priorities.

Principles

The principles underlying the Ecosystem Approach to Environmental Management are as follows:

- The science, decision-making, and program actions that shape environmental management responses will be proactive, well-planned, and undertaken in a systems health context.

- The shared priorities of jurisdictions, sectors, and stakeholders and the added value of collaboration to achieve common objectives will be recognized.

- Specific tasks and areas of business within the broader collective effort will flow to the level or organization that is best positioned to develop or deliver the product, service, or activity.

- Geographic "boundaries" are not mandated; the geographic unit or scale will be set according to scientific, policy, and management requirements and acknowledge the connections between ecosystems.

Investing in the Framework

An overarching framework for an ecosystem approach in Canada requires investment in the following:

Understanding

- Ecosystem structure and processes and the influence of human-induced actions upon them, at large spatial and temporal scale.

- The status and trends of ecosystem structures and processes in general and how to apply the data from this understanding to specific ecosystems under stress.

Decision-making

- At the national level—through a forum(s) or a process(es) bringing together governments and key stakeholders to discuss the status of Canadian ecosystems and to organize and prioritize collective responses.

- At the federal government level—through a decision-making framework and process facilitating and requiring consideration of ecological function and processes.

- At the departmental level (Environment Canada)—through internal governance processes and organization focusing departmental priorities and resources on ecosystem integrity.

Program delivery

- Mechanisms focusing programs (not only national ones) on priority ecosystems and in such a way that the roles and contributions of the programs best deliver agreed-upon results to these locations.

A Final Word

An ecosystem approach to environmental management is based on shifts in understanding, decision-making, and program delivery as shown below:

From environmental management that	To environmental management that
Views the environment as a single issue	Also takes into account economic and social aspects
Involves small spatial scales	Involves multiple scales (ecosystem)
Focuses on one sector	Encompasses many sectors, activities, and users
Has a short-term perspective	Has long-term sustainable goals
Intervenes for specific species or outcomes	Addresses the whole ecosystem

The shift in approach to the environmental management that Environment Canada is proposing will not be easy or quick. Implementing a framework requires changing long-established institutional arrangements; this will take time and sustained leadership and will have resource implications (shifted or new). Implementing the framework does not just involve a "to-do list" for the federal government. An ecosystem approach to environmental management for Canada is a national strategy that has implications for all partners—federal, provincial, and non-governmental.

The Ecosystem Approach: International Dimensions

Ole Hendrickson Scientific Advisor, Biodiversity Convention Office
Environment Canada, Gatineau, QC

INTRODUCTION

Canada is a leader in the development and application of the ecosystem approach, particularly in forested landscapes. Many governments have committed to the implementation of such approaches within their jurisdiction. For example, the British Columbia Minister of Agriculture and Lands recently characterized ecosystem-based management as an "approach to sustainable stewardship of natural resources that is world class" and that ensures a "balance between healthy ecosystems and vibrant communities" (Government of British Columbia 2007).

Canada's successes have helped persuade the international community to endorse the ecosystem approach at the World Summit on Sustainable Development; in agreements and resolutions on agriculture, fisheries, and forests; and in decisions taken under the Convention on Biological Diversity (CBD). The Convention on Biological Diversity decisions acknowledge a particularly close relationship between the ecosystem approach and sustainable forest management.

Among the aims of the May 2007 workshop on "Sectors across Forested Landscapes: Sustainable Systems through Integration and Innovation" were to

- contribute to the implementation of the ecosystem approach in Canada's forests, and

- develop input for Canada's position regarding the ecosystem approach at the 12th meeting of the CBD's Subsidiary Body on Scientific, Technical and Technological Advice (SBSTTA-12).

In this paper, I review international dimensions of the ecosystem approach and discuss prospects for its wider application, drawing in particular on work done under the CBD (CBD 2003, 2004).

HISTORY OF THE ECOSYSTEM APPROACH

The Convention on the Conservation of Antarctic Marine Living Resources (CCAMLR 1982), which came into force in 1982, is viewed as the first international agreement incorporating an ecosystem approach. Its objective is conservation (including sustainable use) of Antarctic marine living resources. The CCAMLR uses a precautionary approach to minimize risk that harvests may prove unsustainable owing to ecosystem variability. It takes into account both natural and human-induced variability, ecological interactions among species, and conservation of all species (not just fish). Similar approaches have been used in the 1995 UN Fish Stocks Assessment (UNGA 1995) and the Reykjavik Declaration on Responsible Fisheries (FAO 2001).

The Food and Agriculture Organization of the United Nations (FAO) has promoted an ecosystem approach in all its areas of expertise, including agriculture, forestry, and fisheries. For example, the Commission on Genetic Resources for Food and Agriculture encouraged countries "to develop strategies, programmes and plans for agrobiodiversity in conformity with an ecosystem approach" (FAO 1997).

Sustainable forest management (SFM) can be viewed as "a means of applying the ecosystem approach to forests" (CBD 2004). The origins of SFM can be traced to the "Forest Principles" (UNGA 1992) adopted at the 1992 Rio Earth Summit and to the work of the International Tropical Timber Organization (ITTO).

Sustainable forest management has been elaborated through criteria and indicators initiatives facilitated by ITTO, FAO, and others. Of particular importance to Canada are the Montréal Process criteria (Table 1) and indicators for boreal and temperate forests, and the Santiago Declaration endorsing them (MPCI 1995).

Table 1. Montréal Process criteria for sustainable forest management.

1. Conservation of biological diversity (specifically ecosystem, species, and genetic diversity).
2. Maintenance of productive capacity of forest ecosystems.
3. Maintenance of forest ecosystem health and vitality (focusing primarily on direct and indirect impacts of human activities on forest structure and functioning).
4. Conservation and maintenance of soil and water resources.
5. Maintenance of forest contribution to global carbon cycle.
6. Maintenance and enhancement of long-term multiple socioeconomic benefits to meet the needs of societies (specifically in relation to production and consumption (of forest goods and services); recreation and tourism; investment in the forest sector; cultural, social and spiritual needs and values; employment and community needs)
7. Legal, institutional, and economic frameworks for forest conservation and sustainable management (including the capacity to undertake measurement, monitoring, research, and development).

Sustainable forest management has been extensively applied in operational settings, drawing on these criteria and indicators, and is more mature than the ecosystem approach in this sense. The 6th Conference of the Parties (COP6) of the CBD observed that, based on SFM experience, "there is a clear need for the ecosystem approach to adopt processes that are based upon clear statements of visions, objectives, and goals for defined regions or issues, thereby becoming more outcome-oriented." Conversely, COP6 noted that "cross-sectoral integration is largely missing from SFM." It suggested that both SFM and the ecosystem approach should state the "inter-generational obligation to sustain the provision of ecosystem goods and services" (CBD 2004).

The Plan of Implementation of the 2002 World Summit on Sustainable Development (WSSD 2002) refers to the ecosystem approach in both specific and general contexts. Paragraphs 30 and 32 of the Plan encourage its application in sustainable development of the oceans, noting the Reykjavik Declaration (FAO 2001) and decision V/6 of the CBD's Conference of the Parties (CBD

2000). Paragraph 44 calls for "wide implementation and further development of the ecosystem approach," as being elaborated in the ongoing work of the CBD. Paragraph 70, in the section on Sustainable Development for Africa, identifies as a priority "Establishing and supporting national and cross-border conservation areas to promote ecosystem conservation according to the ecosystem approach, and to promote sustainable tourism."

Most recently, the 61st session of the UN General Assembly welcomed a report (UNGA 2006) containing "agreed consensual elements relating to ecosystem approaches and oceans" (Table 2). It recalled that states

Table 2. Description of the ecosystem approach in United Nations General Assembly resolution 61/222, Oceans and the law of the sea.

States are invited to consider that an ecosystem approach should:
1. Emphasize conservation of ecosystem structures, functioning, and key processes to maintain ecosystem goods and services.
2. Be applied within geographically specific areas based on ecological criteria.
3. Emphasize the interactions among the components of the ecosystem and between human activities and the ecosystem and among ecosystems.
4. Take into account factors originating outside the boundaries of the defined management area that may influence marine ecosystems in the management area.
5. Strive to balance diverse societal objectives.
6. Be inclusive, with stakeholder and local communities' participation in planning, implementation, and management.
7. Be based on best available knowledge, including traditional, indigenous, and scientific information and be adaptable to new knowledge and experience.
8. Assess risks, and apply the precautionary approach.
9. Use integrated decision-making processes and management related to multiple activities and sectors.
10. Seek to restore degraded marine ecosystems where possible.
11. Assess the cumulative impacts of multiple human activities on marine ecosystems.
12. Take into account ecological, social, cultural, economic, legal, and technical perspectives.
13. Seek the appropriate balance between, and integration of, conservation and sustainable use of marine biological diversity.
14. Seek to minimize adverse impacts of human activities on marine ecosystems and biodiversity, in particular rare and fragile marine ecosystems.

should be guided in applying ecosystem approaches by the Convention on the Law of the Sea (including its implementing agreements, such as the UN Fish Stocks Agreement) and by the CBD, and that the World Summit on Sustainable Development calls for the application of an ecosystem approach by 2010 (UNGA 2007).

THE CONVENTION ON BIOLOGICAL DIVERSITY AND THE ECOSYSTEM APPROACH

At its second meeting, the CBD's Conference of the Parties affirmed that "conservation and sustainable use of biological diversity and its components should be addressed in a holistic manner," and "the ecosystem approach should be the primary framework for action under the Convention" (CBD 1995). Every COP since COP2 has referenced the ecosystem approach in its decisions.

The 3rd COP called for a work program for forest biological diversity that would facilitate the application and integration of the CBD's objectives "in the sustainable management of forests at the national, regional and global levels, in accordance with the ecosystem approach" (CBD 1996). The 4th COP acknowledged the ecosystem approach as a framework for elaboration and implementation of all the various thematic and cross-cutting work programs under the Convention, but also recognized the need for a "workable description and further elaboration of the ecosystem approach" (CBD 1998).

The 5th COP described the ecosystem approach as "a strategy for the integrated management of land, water and living resources that promotes conservation and sustainable use in an equitable way" (CBD 2000). It endorsed 12 principles (Table 3) and 5 points of operational guidance and called on countries and international organizations, "as appropriate," to

- apply the ecosystem approach, giving consideration to the principles and guidance; and

- develop practical expressions of the approach for national policies and legislation and for appropriate implementation activities.

Countries characterized these principles, guidance, and description as "the present level of common understanding," and encouraged "further conceptual elaboration and practical verification."

Table 3. Principles of the Convention on Biological Diversity's ecosystem approach (also known as the "Malawi Principles").

The following 12 principles are complementary and interlinked:
1. The objectives of management of land, water, and living resources are a matter of societal choices.
2. Management should be decentralized to the lowest appropriate level.
3. Ecosystem managers should consider the effects (actual or potential) of their activities on adjacent and other ecosystems.
4. Recognizing potential gains from management, there is usually a need to understand and manage the ecosystem in an economic context. Any such ecosystem-management program should • reduce those market distortions that adversely affect biological diversity; • align incentives to promote biodiversity conservation and sustainable use; • internalize costs and benefits in the given ecosystem to the extent feasible.
5. Conservation of ecosystem structure and functioning, in order to maintain ecosystem services, should be a priority target of the ecosystem approach.
6. Ecosystems must be managed within the limits of their functioning.
7. The ecosystem approach should be undertaken at the appropriate spatial and temporal scales.
8. Recognizing the varying temporal scales and lag-effects that characterize ecosystem processes, objectives for ecosystem management should be set for the long term.
9. Management must recognize that change is inevitable.
10. The ecosystem approach should seek the appropriate balance between, and integration of, conservation and use of biological diversity.
11. The ecosystem approach should consider all forms of relevant information, including scientific, indigenous, and local knowledge, innovations, and practices.
12. The ecosystem approach should involve all relevant sectors of society and scientific disciplines.

The 6th COP noted that implementation of the ecosystem approach has been slow in many countries (CBD 2002). It asked the CBD's executive secretary to convene a meeting of experts who would be asked to

- compare the ecosystem approach with sustainable forest management and develop proposals for their integration; and

- develop proposals for the refinement of the principles and operational guidance of the ecosystem approach on the basis of case studies and lessons learned.

The experts recommended that the existing principles be retained, but provided an annotated rationale and set of implementation guidelines for each.

The 7th COP welcomed the implementation guidelines and annotated rationales that emerged from the meeting of experts (CBD 2004). Countries agreed that "the priority at this time should be on facilitating the implementation of the ecosystem approach" and that "a potential revision of the principles of the ecosystem approach should take place only at a later stage." Countries qualified their support for the ecosystem approach at COP7, stating that its "scale of application" should be decided according to their needs and circumstances.

REVIEW OF THE ECOSYSTEM APPROACH

The 7th COP also decided that an in-depth review of the application of the ecosystem approach would take place at COP9 in May 2008. In preparation for this review, it requested the CBD Secretariat, countries, and relevant international and regional organizations "assess the implementation of the ecosystem approach." At its 12th meeting, the CBD's Subsidiary Body on Scientific, Technical and Technological Advice prepared a recommendation (SBSTTA 2007) for consideration by COP9, based on inputs from countries and relevant organizations summarized in a paper drafted by the CBD Secretariat.

At SBSTTA-12, it was recommended that COP9 urge countries and relevant organizations "as appropriate, and subject to funding and availability of technical capacity" to

- strengthen the promotion of the ecosystem approach in ongoing communication, education, and public awareness activities;

- promote its use in all sectors and enhance inter-sectoral cooperation;

- promote the establishment of concrete national and/ or regional initiatives and pilot projects;

- implement capacity-building initiatives;

- continue submitting case studies and lessons learned and provide further technical input to the CBD's ecosystem approach "Source Book";

- facilitate the full and effective participation of indigenous and local communities in developing tools and mechanisms for its application; and

- strengthen and promote its use for formulation of national biodiversity strategies and action plans and in other relevant policy mechanisms.

In addition to the substantive paragraph summarized above, the SBSTTA-12 recommendation contains a paragraph with a "range of views" to be brought to the attention of COP9. This paragraph was intensely negotiated. Some key phrases were deleted during negotiations including "the ecosystem approach can be applied at many different scales and under very diverse circumstances," a reference to "adaptive management," and "the ecosystem approach… should be more widely adopted in development planning." At SBSTTA-12, it was observed that "the full application of the approach in all of its ecological, social, economic, cultural and political dimensions remains a formidable task, particularly at the larger scale."

Developing countries continue to have serious reservations about the ecosystem approach. Brazil, in particular, wishes to downgrade the status of the ecosystem approach from the "primary framework for action under the Convention" to one among many "tools" for its implementation. Nigeria made the surprising assertion that international agreement to use the ecosystem approach is lacking as it is only a concept. Their interventions provided few clues about the substantive nature of the concerns of developing countries. They may reflect a general reluctance to adopt language that could affect their "sovereign right to exploit their own resources pursuant to their own environmental policies" (CBD, Article 3).

The SBSTTA often resembles a politically based negotiating forum more than a scientific and technical advisory body. Few countries made interventions at SBSTTA-12 on technical aspects of application of the ecosystem approach, even though progress is needed in certain areas (for example, understanding of sustainability thresholds, and the role of ecosystem status monitoring in adaptive management). Open dialogue on the strengths and weaknesses of the ecosystem approach could be instructive. Focusing on a specific geographic area in applying the ecosystem approach is both a strength (people live and use resources in that area) and a weakness (life cycle considerations related to resources removed from or imported to that area are ignored).

Although there may be merit in additional technical discussions related to the ecosystem approach, most observers believe that there is ample guidance and implementation is the priority. More case studies of successful applications could help convince skeptics of the merits of the ecosystem approach.

REFERENCES

[CBD] Convention on Biological Diversity. 1995. Conference of the Parties. Decision II/8. Preliminary consideration of components of biological diversity particularly under threat and action which could be taken under the Convention. http://www.cbd.int/decisions/cop-02.shtml?m=COP-02&id=7081&lg=0 [Accessed November 2007.]

[CBD] Convention on Biological Diversity. 1996. Conference of the Parties. Decision III/12. Programme of work for terrestrial biological diversity: forest biological diversity. http://www.cbd.int/decisions/cop-03.shtml?m=COP-03&id=7108&lg=0 [Accessed November 2007.]

[CBD] Convention on Biological Diversity. 1998. Conference of the Parties. Decision IV/1. Report and recommendations of the third meeting of the SBSTTA, and instructions by the COP to the SBSTTA. http://www.cbd.int/decisions/cop-04.shtml?m=COP-04&id=7124&lg=0 [Accessed November 2007.]

[CBD] Convention on Biological Diversity. 2000. Conference of the Parties. Decision V/6. Ecosystem approach. http://www.cbd.int/decisions/cop-05.shtml?m=COP-05&id=7148&lg=0 [Accessed November 2007.]

[CBD] Convention on Biological Diversity. 2002. Conference of the Parties. Decision VI/12. Ecosystem approach. http://www.cbd.int/decisions/cop-06.shtml?m=COP-06&id=7186&lg=0 [Accessed November 2007.]

[CBD] Convention on Biological Diversity. 2003. Comparison of the conceptual basis of the ecosystem approach in relation to the concept of sustainable forest management UNEP/CBD/EM-EA/1/6. http://www.cbd.int/doc/meetings/esa/ecosys-01/official/ecosys-01-06-en.doc [Accessed November 2007.]

[CBD] Convention on Biological Diversity. 2004. Conference of the Parties. Decision VII/11. Ecosystem approach. http://www.cbd.int/decisions/cop-07.shtml?m=COP-07&id=7748&lg=0 [Accessed November 2007.]

[CCAMLR] Convention on the Conservation of Antarctic Marine Living Resources. 1982. http://www.ccamlr.org/pu/e/gen-intro.htm [Accessed November 2007.]

[FAO] Food and Agriculture Organization of the United Nations. 1997. Report of the Commission on Genetic Resources for Food and Agriculture. Seventh Session, Rome, 15–23 May, 1997. CGRFA-7/97/REP. http://www.fao.org/ag/AGp/AGPS/Pgrfa/pdf/7_97REM.PDF [Accessed November 2007.]

[FAO] Food and Agriculture Organization of the United Nations. 2001. Reykjavik Conference on Responsible Fisheries in the Marine Ecosystem. Thirty-first Session, Rome, 2–13 Nov., 2001. C 2001/INF/25. http://www.fao.org/docrep/meeting/004/Y2211e.htm [Accessed November 2007.]

Government of British Columbia. 2007. News Release. B.C. leads the world in ecosystem-based management. Ministry of Agriculture and Lands and Nanwakolas Council. http://www2.news.gov.bc.ca/news_releases_2005-2009/2007AL0038-000974.htm [Accessed November 2007.]

[MPCI] Montréal Process Criteria and Indicators. 1995. Criteria and Indicators for the Conservation and Sustainable Management of Temperate and Boreal Forests. http://www.rinya.maff.go.jp/mpci/rep-pub/1995/santiago_e.html [Accessed November 2007.]

[SBSTTA] Subsidiary Body on Scientific, Techical and Technological Advice. 2007. Recommendation XII/1 adopted by the SBSTTA at its twelfth meeting: Application of the ecosystem approach. http://www.cbd.int/recommendations [Accessed November 2007]

[UNGA] United Nations General Assembly. 1992. Non-Legally Binding Authoritative Statement of Principles for a Global Consensus on the Management, Conservation and Sustainable Development of All Types of Forests. Document A/CONF.151/26 (Vol. III). http://www.un.org/documents/ga/conf151/aconf15126-3annex3.htm [Accessed November 2007.]

[UNGA] United Nations General Assembly. 1995. Agreement for the Implementation of the Provisions of the United Nations Convention on the Law of the Sea of 10 December 1982 Relating to the Conservation and Management of Straddling Fish Stocks and Highly Migratory Fish Stocks. Document A/CONF.164/37. http://www.un.org/Depts/los/convention_agreements/texts/fish_stocks_agreement/CONF164_37.htm [Accessed November 2007.]

[UNGA] United Nations General Assembly. 2006. Report on the work of the United Nations Open-ended Informal Consultative Process on Oceans and the Law of the Sea at its seventh meeting. Document A/61/156. http://www.un.org/ga/61/documentation/list.shtml [Accessed November 2007.]

[UNGA] United Nations General Assembly. 2007. Resolution 61/222 adopted by the United Nations General Assembly. Oceans and the law of the sea. Document A/RES/61/222 http://www.un.org/Depts/dhl/resguide/r61.htm [Accessed November 2007.]

[WSSD] World Summit on Sustainable Development. 2002. Plan of Implementation of the World Summit on Sustainable Development. http://www.un.org/esa/sustdev/documents/WSSD_POI_PD/English/WSSD_PlanImpl.pdf [Accessed November 2007.]

Ecosystem-based Approaches to Species at Risk

Tom J. Fowler Senior Advisor, Species of Concern, Oceans Directorate
Oceans and Habitat Sector, Fisheries and Oceans Canada, Ottawa, ON

INTRODUCTION

Complementing existing provincial endangered species legislation and consistent with commitments made under the 1996 Federal–Provincial Accord for the Protection of Endangered Wildlife in Canada, the federal *Species at Risk Act* (SARA) came fully into force in 2004. Since that time, approximately 400 species have been listed as either endangered or threatened, most of which were transferred to the "legal" list from a pre-existing list of species designated at-risk by the Committee on the Status of Endangered Wildlife in Canada (COSEWIC). That committee was given a legal basis under the act in recognition of the work it has undertaken assessing species since the 1970s.

Under the act, designation as endangered or threatened carries with it the obligation for governments and stakeholders to put in place measures to protect the species, its critical habitat, and its residence (if applicable) from identified threats, and to put in place a recovery strategy with objectives established for its recovery. Considering the lengthy (and growing) list of species, the focus on landscapes and habitat, there has been considerable interest in exploring ways to view species assessment and recovery through an ecosystem lens.

SARA ASSESSMENT AND RECOVERY CYCLE AND ECOSYSTEM APPROACHES

The assessment of a species at risk includes an evaluation of species abundance, distribution, habitat quantification, and threats to the species and its habitat. This work is coordinated by COSEWIC and undertaken by government and non-government experts in a variety of fields. Once completed, COSEWIC submits a status report to the government and a recommendation is sent from the responsible department (Environment Canada or Fisheries and Oceans Canada) to the Governor in Council who makes the final decision on whether or not to add the species to the "legal" list.

If listed, the SARA prohibitions against killing or harming the species or destroying its critical habitat come into place, along with other mandatory, time-bound requirements including the establishment of recovery strategies. Assessment informs recovery through processes such as Recovery Potential Assessment and the identification of critical habitat, among others. Recovery informs assessment through such means as species monitoring, establishment of research priorities, and investigations to determine the severity and likelihood of impact from identified threats. Thus it is a cycle.

There are opportunities to pursue an ecosystem approach throughout the SARA. The single-species work undertaken by universities, government scientists, and others in collaboration with COSEWIC examines and quantifies habitat dependencies, species interactions, etc., and in many ways, it is this community of species experts that have formed the foundation for ecosystem science as it relates to biodiversity conservation. Similarly, the recovery teams engaged in on-going protection and recovery of listed species invest much effort and resources on abatement of threats that affect multiple species, and the preservation of habitat that benefits multiple species. As scientists and managers contemplate appropriate recovery objectives for listed species (and appropriate management objectives for exploited commercial species), a key question that has emerged is, What population size allows this species to maintain its role in the ecosystem?

Multispecies-based and Ecosystem-based Approaches to Recovery

In multispecies-based approaches, recovery actions focus on common threats faced by multiple species at risk. Ecosystem-based approaches require an ecologically defined area, habitat, or ecosystem type. Recovery actions focus on interactions among species, the maintenance of major ecosystem processes, and protection of physical features.

Multispecies-based and ecosystem-based approaches are extensions of the single-species models. Good single-species assessments and recovery strategies do consider basic ecological parameters like competition, habitat dependency, predation, etc., as well as broad spectrum threats faced by multiple species.

In the context of SARA, there is considerable value in formalizing multispecies and ecosystem approaches when designing recovery strategies. SARA's strict timelines for posting recovery strategies, and the fact that assessed species are submitted individually to government, can preclude the development of multispecies-based or ecosystem-based recovery strategies. But the act provides more flexible timelines for action plans (which put recovery strategies into operation). Thus, one way for the recovery planning community to move forward with these approaches is to create multispecies-based and ecosystem-based action plans based on single-species recovery strategies.

The Oceans Directorate of Fisheries and Oceans Canada hosted a workshop in March 2006 in collaboration with recovery practitioners from across Canada to look at these approaches (Gardner 2006). It provided detailed guidance on when and how to use the various approaches.

There is clear legislative and policy direction in support of an ecosystem approach. It is clearly referenced in the federal *Species at Risk Act* as well as the federal–provincial RENEW Recovery Handbook (National Recovery Working Group 2005). Several recent scientific papers have concluded that there are benefits to be achieved. A prominent organization within the NGO community came to a more cautious conclusion, "[these] approaches

seem intuitively…a holistic way of approaching SAR recovery [but] effectiveness of multi-species planning has yet to be assessed [and] knowledge gaps [re.] ecosystem level research [are such that] ecosystem recovery strategies may not be practical" (Sheppard et al. 2005). One concern is that although these approaches may be effective to help a group of species, they may prove insufficient to recover individual species. This is particularly the case for species in imminent risk of extinction, in which case a single-species approach would likely make more sense.

The most commonly noted benefits and limitations of ecosystems or multispecies approaches follow:

Expected advantages	Challenges
Identifies root causes of species imperilment	Limited experience
Allows management at the appropriate scale	Conflicts with tight SARA time frames
Integrates with diverse planning processes	Complex recovery goals
Benefits non-listed species	Increased resources (short term)
Identifies conflicting species needs	SARA requires threats focused on throughout species range
Fewer strategies and plans to prepare	Unrealistic expectations

Conclusions

Although ecosystem and multispecies approaches are not new concepts, they have rarely been applied to SARA implementation in a formal, documented fashion. One exception is the Sydenham River Ecosystem Recovery Strategy (Dextrase et al. 2003), an excellent example of producing multiple benefits by protecting an ecologically defined area. Another is the multispecies action plan for large whales in Pacific Canadian waters (Spaven et al. 2006), where similarities among various species and their key threats naturally led to a significant degree of collaboration among scientists and recovery practitioners. Eventually, in the action planning stage, this culminated in the development of a joint action plan where whale research agendas, monitoring, enforcement, and other major recovery efforts were undertaken and formally documented. A key lesson is that where efficiencies and/or effectiveness can be realized, this should be pursued in a structured way. Recovery resources are limited, as is the expertise that must be brought to bear on the most significant threats to Canada's species.

Another concluding point relates to the idea of "role of species in the ecosystem" concept mentioned. Pursuant to the *Oceans Act* of 1997, the Government of Canada's Oceans Action Plan has led to the identification of five Large Oceans Management Areas, covering significant areas within each of Canada's three oceans. These areas have been extensively studied. Comprehensive Ecosystem Overview Reports and Ecosystem Assessment Reports have been developed for each. Smaller Ecologically Significant Areas have been identified, as have Ecologically Significant Species (ESS). There is a natural linkage between SARA Recovery Strategies and the science and management efforts that are being brought to bear on ESS. A key conclusion is that policy makers must come to terms with two apparently divergent acts. SARA identifies (or lists) species based on risk of extinction, whereas the *Oceans Act* lists species based on role in the ecosystem. However, with some forward thinking, several convergences between the two acts will likely emerge to demonstrate that the two are in fact complementary.

REFERENCES

Dextrase, A.J.; Staton, S.K; Metcalfe-Smith, J.L. 2003. National Recovery Strategy for Species at Risk in the Sydenham River: an ecosystem approach. National Recovery Plan No. 25. Recovery of Nationally Endangered Wildlife (RENEW), Ottawa, ON. 73 p.

Gardner, J. 2006. Workshop on Ecosystem and Multispecies Approaches to the Recovery of Species at Risk, March 1–2, 2006, Vancouver, BC. Proceedings prepared for Fisheries and Oceans Canada by Dovetail Consulting Inc., Vancouver, BC.

National Recovery Working Group. 2005. Recovery handbook (ROMAN). 2005-2006 ed., Oct.2005. Recovery of Nationally Endangered Wildlife (RENEW), Ottawa, ON. 71 p. + appendices.

Sheppard, V.; Rangeley, R.; Laughren, J. 2005. An assessment of multi-species recovery strategies and ecosystem-based approaches for management of marine species at risk in Canada. World Wildlife Fund, Toronto, ON.

Spaven, L.; Gregr, E.J.; Calambokidis, J; Convey, L.; Ford, J.K.B.; Perry, R.I.; Short, C. 2006. Draft Recovery Action Plan for Blue, Fin, Sei, and Right Whales (*Balaenoptera musculus, B. physalus, B. borealis,* and *Eubalaena japonica*) in Pacific Canadian Waters. Fisheries and Oceans Canada, Nanaimo, BC. iii+30 p.

Integrated Landscape Management: Applying Sustainable Development to Land Use

Tony Andrews Executive Director
Prospectors and Developers Association of Canada, Toronto, ON

INTRODUCTION

Sustainable development applied to land use means adopting an effective approach to optimizing environmental, social, and economic priorities on the landscape, and in the specific context of the mining industry, reconciles the needs of conservation of biodiversity and ecosystem function with that of resource development, community priorities, and the needs of other land users.

Traditional approaches to land-use and resource management have not effectively accomplished this objective and have actually contributed to conflict among land users. The underlying cause of this failure is the lack of a true systematic approach underpinned by integration at all levels, including government institutions, polices, regulations, and decision-making, and industry operations on the land. Although Canada is generally viewed as a relatively unspoiled country with large uninhabited areas, competing needs on the land are already causing significant challenges and they are only going to increase in intensity. New approaches are required to reconcile competing needs and to deliver on identified environmental, social, and economic priorities. This can only be accomplished through mechanisms of increased integration and collaboration.

Integrated landscape management (ILM) is a concept that has been quietly developing over the past three decades and together with the recent introduction of sophisticated tools for planning and information management, it offers the potential of accomplishing the integrated, systems approach that is required. But beyond its intellectual and technical elegance, and like the concept of sustainable development itself,

ILM allows people with totally different perspectives and priorities to enter the same tent and engage in dialogue and collaboration on how progress can be made on land-use issues.

However, there are some powerful barriers to making progress and ways must be found to break through them.

THE MINING INDUSTRY'S RELATIONSHIP TO THE LAND

Mining is a major contributor to Canada's economic growth. In 2005 (the latest date for which statistics are available), the mining and mineral processing industries contributed $50.7 billion to the Canadian economy, equal to 4.0% of the country's gross domestic product; employed nearly 400 000 people in 115 communities across Canada, particularly in rural areas and in the North; and was the largest single employer of Aboriginal people.

The mining industry is capital-intensive, high-risk, and, in its initial phases, a major user of the land base. It comprises two subsectors: exploration and mining operations. The industry's use of land in terms of extent and impact is best described by the analogy of a pyramid. The base represents the large quantum of land required for exploration purposes; at this stage, there is minimal impact on the ecosystem. As the industry progresses toward the apex of the pyramid through the stages of the mining cycle—prospecting, advanced exploration, mine development, mine operation, and closure—the extent of land required diminishes significantly, but the potential impact on ecosystems increases.

Exploration is a sophisticated, high-technology, capital-intensive activity. Investment in exploration can amount to $10 million–$100 million depending on many factors, including the size and location of the project. Uncertainty, however, is endemic to exploration activity. Only 1 in every 100 projects progresses to the advanced stage, and only 1 in every 1000 projects results in mine development and operation. Given a successful discovery, the entire process from discovery to mine production can take from 7 to 12 years.

Clearly, because the industry requires access to large amounts of land at the initial exploration stage, and because it requires a heavy infusion of capital before an operating mine produces financial returns for its owners, long-term employment for local communities, and tax revenues to governments, land and resource management is extremely important. It must be clear and predictable, allowing the industry a high level of confidence that public priorities will be met effectively.

Old and New Thinking on Land-Use Issues

Not too long ago, resource industries and conservation groups were in intense conflict and debate over land-use issues, and the lightning rod was the use of protected areas to achieve conservation objectives. Industry accepted protected areas as one mechanism to achieve preservation of discrete, highly sensitive areas but criticized what it thought was an inappropriate application of a single-tool approach taken by conservation groups and governments at the time to achieving broad conservation objectives. Given that biodiversity and ecosystem functions are dynamic and occur over broad landscapes, industry had no confidence that an overreliance on protected areas of fixed location and size would effectively achieve the broad conservation objectives identified. As well, protected areas alienated land that contained mineral resources valued by the mining industry and by society.

However, there was accumulating evidence of the degradation of ecosystem function and habitat; there was a fear that development was unconstrained; there was a lack of trust that government and industry would take responsible action to mitigate undesired impacts, and protected areas became a kind of insurance policy against the worst-case scenarios. Also, no one had any alternative models to suggest; therefore all were stuck in the "protected areas paradigm" making very little progress.

Over the past six years, there has been a lull in the rhetoric and conflict, and conservation and resource industry groups, along with government representatives, have been initiating dialogue. The arguments and debates have moved from broad, strongly held positions to more specific levels of detail and in many cases to the application of science; new planning concepts and tools have been developed including scenario modeling techniques and the application of ecosystem thresholds, all of which add up to a positive evolution. However, the key question is, How has this progress in relationships, new tools, and knowledge translated to real progress on the landscape?

There has indeed been some progress toward better land and resource management in a broad sense through programs such as the Canadian Biodiversity Strategy, the National Forest Strategy, the Model Forest Program, and more regional programs such as the Prairie Conservation Action Plan, the NorSask Project, and the current ILM initiative in Alberta (see Seiferling, this publication). However, there has been a failure to make significant progress on the development and application of a systematic approach to land and resource management in Canada that incorporates the level of integration, community engagement, temporal and spatial planning, and management of cumulative effects that is really needed. Progress has been frustratingly slow and incremental—it has been a dance that has involved as many steps sideways and backward as there have been forward.

There has been no long-term commitment to ILM. Governments and industry have adopted some of its elements, but no one has put a full system into operation. Integration will not work unless that happens. As a result, we are still dealing with planning and decision-making systems that are fragmented, incremental, and divided along sectoral lines.

There are several barriers that are preventing progress, the most important of which are institutional, primarily in government but also among industry sectors. Another barrier is capacity. Our available capacity is often completely invested in existing endeavors and there is very little to direct toward new initiatives such as ILM. The requirement for new sources of capacity and collaboration is discussed further in the following.

Toward a New Approach

Many are now convinced that the only way forward is to think in terms of entire landscapes and to broaden our concepts of land and resources in terms of space and time. There are compelling reasons for this:

1. First and most obvious, ecosystems and ecosystem functions exist over broad areas of space and time and require approaches that reflect these fundamental realities.

2. The landscape and ecosystem function are a dynamic system manifested by forest succession and the movement of old-growth areas over time; management systems therefore would work best if they were designed to be flexible and adaptive as opposed to being rigid.

3. Forest succession rates are measured in time frames of 10s to 100s of years, and we need to understand how the decisions we are making now will affect the landscape in the distant future.

4. Cumulative effects is an orphaned concept—we know that it is a crucial aspect of land and resource management that we should be applying—but it simply will not fit easily into present land-use decision-making systems.

5. Canada's sheer size and remoteness, at one time, was considered a means of protection. Because of modern technology, development can now take place anywhere.

6. Already there are regions of Canada that are dealing with very significant land-use challenges and Alberta is a prime example. Water problems in the south and intense land use in the north have caused Alberta to become host to some of the leading advocates of ILM in the country.

7. Aboriginal people live in the remote regions of Canada where much of the resource industries conduct their work. They no longer think in terms of the immediate surroundings of the community, but in terms of large areas referred to as traditional lands.

Promise and Potential of Integrated Landscape Management Approach

The Prospectors and Developers Association of Canada (PDAC) recognized the potential of ILM in the latter part of the 1990s and thereafter conducted research and met with experts working on various aspects of the "ecosystem approach" as it was formerly known. In 2001, the PDAC developed a land-use strategy that was underpinned by a commitment to furthering the development and acceptance of ILM. In 2003, the PDAC, in partnership with Wildlife Habitat Canada and the Biodiversity Convention Office of Environment Canada, organized an experts workshop on ILM, the objectives of which were to agree on a definition, recognize the opportunities and barriers regarding moving forward, and identify next steps.

The formation of the Canadian Coalition for Integrated Landscape Management (CCILM) in 2003 was an outcome of this workshop. As mentioned previously, ILM is a concept that allows all parties into the tent to discuss, debate, and collaborate on establishing a better approach to land-use management and resource use. The CCILM is an excellent example.

The coalition includes representatives from national associations and individual companies of the forestry, energy, and mining industries, conservation interests, academia, provincial and federal governments, and Aboriginal peoples. Beginning in 2003, it has met frequently to develop the concept of ILM, to increase awareness about it, and to advocate for its adoption.

In 2005, the coalition published a technical paper on ILM, copies of which are available on the PDAC Web site (http://www.pdac.ca/pdac/advocacy/land-use/ilm-concept-paper.pdf). This paper defines the ILM system, its principles, functional components, benefits, and means of implementation. A description of the key elements follows.

Integrated Landscape Management System Defined

ILM allows society to set and achieve objectives at scales appropriate for ecosystems and decision-making. ILM involves the consolidation of current, independent sector-based approaches (species-based, habitat-based, or protected areas-based management approaches) into a more encompassing framework for the long-term maintenance of ecosystems and the sustainable use of resources. The operative word is integration which should replace the existing reality of fragmentation.

The basic principles of a properly designed ILM system may be summarized as follows:

1. **Integration:** Current systems are fragmented both within government where decisions are made along sectoral lines, and in terms of operations, whereby various industries go about their business on the ground oblivious of one another. Integration is required vertically along the stages of planning and decision-making from the broad policy level to specific management of projects on the ground, and integration is required horizontally across government departments, sectors, and land uses;

2. **Planning at Appropriate Scales:** ILM approaches planning from the point of view of whole landscapes and time frames, beginning at a very large scale and moving sequentially lower as required. Thus objectives are achieved over spatial and temporal scales relevant to ecosystem patterns and decision-making needs;

3. **Inclusivity:** Decisions about economic, social, and environmental aspects of land and resource uses involve **trade-offs** and therefore must be appropriately informed and must rely on input from communities of interest at all levels;

4. And it is **Adaptive:** It is a continuous learning process that is flexible, allowing effective management responses to changing conditions and information, whether that information comes from research or the sites of operations.

Some of the key elements of an ILM system that allow it to function include:

1. **Scenario Modeling:** Computer-based modeling systems that combine non-spatial, spatial, and animation capacities to project the consequences of today's decisions into the future, so that preferred options can be made in the most informed manner.

2. The Application of **thresholds:** Benchmark indicators that are used to estimate the limit or capacity of an ecosystem to accommodate land-use activities and still function sustainably.

3. **Research, Monitoring, and Data Management:** Provide new information by tracking and evaluating performance against objectives, and facilitate access to the best available data for informed decisions and feedback into the adaptive management process.

4. **Risk Assessment and Cumulative Effects Management:** All of the previous elements allow for the effective implementation of risk assessment and provide the framework for cumulative effects management.

5. **Conservation Planning:** Within the ILM system, a conservation framework can be developed that is tailored to the needs of the landscape being considered and uses an array of conservation tools (including protected areas) selected to most effectively achieve those objectives.

Because ILM is an adaptive process, it can be implemented now before the working model is perfected, applying the principle of adaptive management as it progresses.

CURRENT REALITY AND NEXT STEPS

As the work of the CCILM progresses, there has been growing interest in ILM across Canada. It has been discussed at every venue with a focus on land use, and various aspects of ILM have been the subject of recent workshops hosted by departments of the federal and provincial governments. However, the approach has been fragmented and dispersed and there has been no long-term commitment to ILM. Provincial, territorial, and federal governments have adopted some of its elements and moved partly toward the overall goal, but none has yet committed to putting the full concept into operation. Planning and decision-making systems are still fragmented, incremental, and divided along sectoral lines.

This raises the question, What can be done to affect a breakthrough? The CCILM contemplated several options, one of which was the creation of a Center of Excellence for Land Use and Resource Management whose primary role would be to act as a focal point for all those with an interest in land-use and resource management. It would channel the considerable amount of energy, interest, and expanding body of knowledge that currently exists scattered across Canada into a centralized reservoir. The Center of Excellence would be a meeting place where proponents would share information and knowledge, debate the issues, reach agreement, and provide direction for putting ILM into operation and continuing its development.

The proposed center would incorporate a research function, combining science and policy, to continue the development of the multidimensional scientific needs of ILM and conduct the policy and legislative research to develop the types of institutions that an ILM system requires.

Through all these functions, a Center of Excellence would act as a resource of knowledge and information needs for jurisdictions implementing ILM. At the same time, the jurisdictions themselves would become a valuable source of knowledge, feeding their practical experience back to the center.

There is growing international interest in ILM and its potential benefits, and many countries will be looking to Canada for leadership in developing and adapting the ILM concept. The Center of Excellence could provide the focus and the means for Canada to provide this international leadership.

To become a reality, the Center of Excellence will need long-term commitment and support from the highest levels. This can best be achieved through a high-level leadership council with representation from the resource industries, conservation interests, Aboriginal peoples, academia, and provincial, territorial, and federal governments. Such a council could provide the momentum to put ILM into operation.

CONCLUSION

Canadians want assurances that lands and resources are being managed and used responsibly. Resource industries are looking for an approach to land-use and resource management that is efficient, predictable, and gives them confidence that objectives will be effectively met, including those of conservation. Conservationists are looking for an approach to land-use and resource management that makes ecosystem function and conservation of biodiversity and habitat a priority and provides effective and long-term objectives for accomplishing this. Governments are looking for a policy, planning, and regulatory regime that delivers sustainable development on the landscape that all communities of interest understand and support.

ILM provides the opportunity for achieving these objectives through an integrated, systems approach to optimizing environmental, social, and economic priorities on the landscape. Progress toward implementing fully operating ILM systems on the land will depend on the ability of individual communities of interest to reach beyond their own focused agendas and embark on a process of collaboration.

Tools for Developing Ecosystem-based Approaches

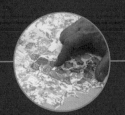

NatureServe Vista: A Decision-Support System for Land-Use Planning and Resource Management

Andy Cutko Forestry Program Officer
NatureServe, Bowdoinham, ME

Patrick Crist Conservation Planning Services Program Manager
NatureServe, Boulder, CO

Steve Curtis Executive Director, Canada Partnerships
NatureServe Canada, Ottawa, ON

INTRODUCTION

Ecosystem-based management approaches will play a vital role in identifying cost-effective solutions to the complex problem of existing and emerging threats to Canada's natural heritage. In this paper, we show how a tool, NatureServe Vista, will help make ecosystem-based management in Canada more effective. We describe its development and how and where it is being used to create, evaluate, implement, and monitor land-use and resource-management plans. We conclude with some advice on ecosystem management.

NATURESERVE

NatureServe is an international organization that strives to provide a scientific basis for effective conservation action. NatureServe and NatureServe Canada work in partnership with member Conservation Data Centres (CDCs) to increase the quality and accessibility of biodiversity data for forest management and planning on public and private lands. More specifically, each of the CDCs regularly supplies biodiversity data to the forest industry to support sustainable forest management, and many of them provide other services including biodiversity inventories, training, ecological classification, and mapping to a variety of clients. The type of data managed by NatureServe is required by two leading forest certification systems, the Sustainable Forestry Initiative and the Forest Stewardship Council.

Cannings et al. (2005) noted that although habitat loss and fragmentation remain the leading threats to Canada's ecosystems, new threats have emerged including invasive species, wildlife diseases, and climate change. Computer-based decision-support systems will be increasingly necessary to help in evaluating options for mitigating the effects of and making informed decisions on these threats. NatureServe has thus collaborated on the development of a network to promote ecosystem-based management tools and to support their use in coastal and marine environments and associated watersheds. The Ecosystem-Based Management Tools Network (http://www.ebmtools.org/index.html) was launched in 2006.

NATURESERVE VISTA

NatureServe Vista is a decision-support tool for ecosystem-based management. This specialized software system guides users through a generic and well-established process for conducting impact assessments and conservation and natural-resource planning.

Objectives

Whether the goal is to revise a forest management plan or to designate how public lands can be used, the environment is shaped by the choices of stakeholders and decision-makers. The challenge is to understand and predict the effects of these choices and harness this knowledge to make land-use and resource-management decisions that enhance the quality of human life while preserving a country's natural heritage. NatureServe Vista enables users to create, evaluate, implement, and monitor land-use and resource-management plans within the context of existing economic, social, and political constraints. It does this by integrating conservation information, natural-resource management practices, and land-use patterns and policies into a single GIS-based decision-support framework.

More specifically, NatureServe Vista's decision-making framework allows users to

- manage projects through their complete lifecycle, including analysis, planning, implementation, and monitoring;

- create land-use or resource-management plans that reflect unique situations and values;

- improve the efficiency of planning processes;

- enhance the consistency and repeatability of planning efforts;

- improve communications and build consensus with interested parties;

- develop documentation that supports land-use or resource-management decisions;

- maximize conservation results with minimum cost and trade-offs; and

- reduce costly legal conflicts.

Application

The steps involved in applying NatureServe Vista summarized below are described in detail on the NatureServe Web site (http://www.natureserve.org/prodServices/vista/overview.jsp).

Identify conservation elements and their values

Users of NatureServe Vista begin by identifying conservation elements in a study area—important biological, cultural, and social features such as rare species and ecosystems, historic sites, and prime agricultural soils. NatureServe Vista rates each element according to its value for conservation (for example, based on global or regional rarity) and generates maps that show where the element is found, the quality of its occurrence (that is, the viability of the population or integrity of the ecosystem), and confidence in the data's accuracy. The resulting map highlights the most valuable places to conserve for each individual element.

Summarize conservation values

NatureServe Vista helps users aggregate the conservation values generated in the previous step from individual elements to broader spatial scales such as watersheds, individual forest stands, or forest planning units. The resulting map shows which areas should be targeted

for conservation and which ones could withstand more intensive use. These "conservation value summary" maps have also been used as cost surfaces—models showing the variation in cost over an area—to aid in landscape planning for commercial or industrial development or utility corridors. Users may customize the depiction on these maps by adjusting the conservation value summaries; for instance, users may choose to

- evaluate a set of conservation elements, such as all species at risk, all species at risk within a particular taxonomic group, or wetland systems with high functional values;

- assign importance weights to individual elements so that conservation objectives, such as conserving rare species or maintaining mature forest stands, can be prioritized; as well, different weighting systems based on features important to certain interest groups could be used and thus conservation priorities for these groups could be compared; and

- identify areas of high ecological integrity or areas where additional surveys or mapping are needed to increase confidence in the data.

Assign conservation goals

To measure and monitor project success, users can assign conservation goals for each conservation element. For example, a practical goal may be to conserve a percentage of the natural boreal forest within a planning unit, or alternatively, conserve all of the populations of the rare showy lady's slipper, *Cypripedium reginae*. Although setting goals is not required, it is useful for determining which elements have received sufficient conservation attention and which ones are particularly at risk. NatureServe Vista outputs enable users to assess progress toward these goals, such as 80% success in boreal forest conservation or 100% success in conservation of showy lady's slippers within the study area.

Evaluate land-use scenarios

NatureServe Vista's Scenario Evaluation feature integrates conservation objectives with socioeconomic factors. For each element previously selected, users assign an expected effect from the land-use and resource-management practices occurring or anticipated for the area. Responses can range from simple binary (compatible/not compatible) to categorical scales. For example, a rare plant population may be considered "incompatible" with a proposed clearcut. Expected effects on the elements can also take the form of a detailed condition-change model that assigns the effect of land uses on a conservation element condition at the site of impact and at a distance from it. Users then import various land-use and resource-management policy scenarios—essentially a series of alternative land-use plans for the planning region—and evaluate the effects of these scenarios against conservation goals. The Scenario Evaluation feature allows users to

- evaluate and compare land-use plans and alternative conservation strategies;

- measure progress against defined conservation goals;

- update land-use scenarios as often as needed with new data or land-use decisions to maintain a baseline scenario of actual land use and policies; and

- track progress toward goals over time.

Generate conservation solutions

NatureServe Vista facilitates the use of two analytical tools, Marxan and SPOT, often used by conservation experts to identify the best areas for conservation based on features to be protected, specific goals, and the expected costs associated with conserving specific locations. With NatureServe Vista, users can more easily develop the inputs required to run these tools and generate conservation solutions. The results from these tools (an optimized set of conservation locations) can then be imported back into NatureServe Vista for further analyses and refinement. When the Marxan/SPOT results are incorporated back into a scenario, they can be more precisely evaluated for their ability to meet goals. With the Site Explorer feature described below, users can also apply the Marxan/SPOT results to guide the development of an action plan that specifies appropriate land-use and management practices, implementation policies, and funding sources.

Explore sites and create mitigation plans

The Site Explorer tool in NatureServe Vista allows users to test possible land-use practices and policies for a site or set of sites and thereby obtain immediate feedback about the ramifications of changes to current practices and policies. Once a site is selected, a user is provided with an inventory of conservation elements, land uses, and policies for that site, the response of the element to the land uses, and the proportion of protection or habitat loss the site is contributing for each element.

Users can then shift to an override mode where they can propose and test alternative land uses and policies for the site.

Documentation Tools

NatureServe Vista provides opportunities to document each step of a planning process, and such documentation is important for tracking progress and retaining a record of the project for an organization. Users may cite references, record assumptions, and document the logic behind each input and decision. This helps users share their knowledge of the planning process and to justify their recommendations and decisions to interested parties.

Standard Reporting Features

NatureServe Vista's reporting features allow users to communicate with decision-makers and constituents via standard reports and maps. NatureServe Vista generates XML reports exportable as HTML files with embedded maps. Reports are available for all elements and analyses. These reports, which are easily published online, can be exported to software programs such as Microsoft Word or Excel. The references, assumptions, and decision points that are captured during the planning process are included in these reports, enhancing the user's ability to communicate the details of decision-making processes.

CASE STUDY: EVALUATING CONSERVATION AND ECONOMIC VALUES ON POTLATCH FOREST LANDS, ARKANSAS

In 2005, NatureServe worked with the Arkansas Natural Heritage Commission (a state agency) and Potlatch Corporation (a forest products company) to evaluate the compatibility of conservation and forest management options on 50 000 ha of privately owned forestland in Arkansas. The study area included stands that were valued both for conservation reasons (for example, the preservation of longleaf pine, *Pinus palustris,* or the red-cockaded woodpecker, *Picoides borealis*) and for economic ones (high timber production). The objectives of the study were to

- identify forest stands that were free of conflict for extraction of forest products, free of conflict for conservation management, or in conflict and requiring additional analyses and management planning, and

- evaluate and demonstrate NatureServe Vista decision-support system capabilities for Potlatch and other partners.

For these analyses, NatureServe used forest stand type polygons (about 5–50 ha in size) as the spatial unit of analysis and categorized conservation values for these stands as low, medium, and high based on the rarity and viability of species or ecological communities associated with these forest stands. Economic value was also categorized (high, medium, or low) for each forest stand based on the existing timber volume. A map with stands classified according to conservation values was then combined with one in which the same stands were rated for economic values. The resulting map of combined values (Figure 1) had nine possible categories of opportunities and conflicts (for example, high conservation value or low economic value). From it, areas of opportunity and conflict could be easily identified and analyzed.

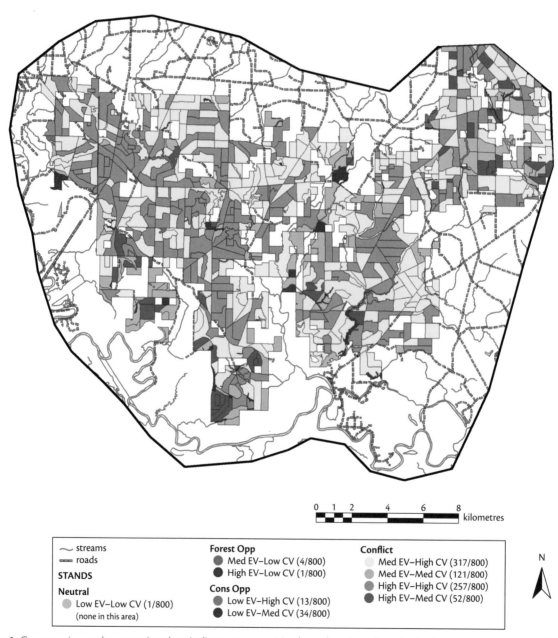

| 0 | 1 | 2 | | 4 | | 6 | | 8 | |
kilometres

| ∼ | streams |
| --- | roads |

STANDS

Neutral
- Low EV–Low CV (1/800)
  (none in this area)

Forest Opp
- Med EV–Low CV (4/800)
- High EV–Low CV (1/800)

Cons Opp
- Low EV–High CV (13/800)
- Low EV–Med CV (34/800)

Conflict
- Med EV–High CV (317/800)
- Med EV–Med CV (121/800)
- High EV–High CV (257/800)
- High EV–Med CV (52/800)

N

Figure 1. Conservation and economic values indicate opportunities (green) and conflicts (red) using one set of conservation data attributes (EV=economic value; CV=conservation value; Med=medium; Cons.=conservation; Opp=opportunity).

NatureServe Vista was also used in this study to determine how four potential stand prescriptions would affect each of 30 or more conservation elements identified for the site:

- **deferred or no cutting** in riparian zones, red-cockaded woodpecker nesting sites, and some wetland forest types;

- **partial harvests** of lowland hardwoods and natural pine stands;

- **biomass harvests** (removal of all stems, then allowing some natural regeneration) of some upland hardwood and mixedwood types; and

- **high-yield prescriptions** (clearcutting, burning, mechanical site preparation, or herbicide application) in plantations and upland natural pine forests.

The model users found, for example, that the deferred/no cutting and partial-harvest options were considered compatible with retention of mature longleaf pine stands, while biomass harvest and high-yield prescriptions were considered incompatible. By assessing the spatial results of these compatibility assignments and comparing the conservation outcomes to the initial conservation goals, the model users were able to test the effects of various stand prescriptions across the landscape in the study area.

CHALLENGES AND OPPORTUNITIES IN ECOSYSTEM MANAGEMENT: A NATURESERVE PERSPECTIVE

The wide variety of projects put forth under the banner of ecosystem-based management suggests there is no single tool or approach that is right for all circumstances.

Nonetheless, long-term success and stakeholder satisfaction may be attained if practitioners

- Establish clear, measurable objectives that can be monitored. These objectives should be articulated in writing and agreed upon by all project participants.

- Ensure that there is the funding and political will to commit to monitoring over a long time period and at a level of intensity that will permit sufficient verification (that is, quantitative monitoring where possible).

- Use the best scientific data available, but make informed and well-documented judgments where data are limited. For many conservation situations, there will never be "perfect" data.

- Recognize complexities in spatial and temporal dimensions. In forestry applications, for example, multiple iterations of NatureServe Vista may be used to portray landscape changes (and associated changes in conservation value) over time.

- Integrate analyses and decisions at multiple scales. In forest and conservation planning, even the broadest landscape-level plans must ultimately be implemented at the stand level; planners and foresters at all levels must agree with the overall plan objectives.

- Ensure that concepts of adaptive management are used appropriately to modify plans according to changing circumstances within the landscape in question and not to realign a well-designed and broadly supported project due to political influences.

REFERENCES

Cannings, S.; Anions, M.F.E.; Rainer, R.; Stein, B.A. 2005. Our home and native land: Canadian species of global conservation concern. NatureServe Canada, Ottawa, ON. 44 p.

An Integrated Risk Analysis Framework in Support of Sustainable Forest Management in Canada: Project Overview

Brian J. Hearn Forest Wildlife Ecologist, Atlantic Forestry Centre
Canadian Forest Service, Natural Resources Canada, Corner Brook, NL

Joan E. Luther Research Scientist, Atlantic Forestry Centre
Canadian Forest Service, Natural Resources Canada, Corner Brook, NL

David R. Gray Disturbance Ecologist, Atlantic Forestry Centre
Canadian Forest Service, Natural Resources Canada, Fredericton, NB

INTRODUCTION

Ensuring forest sustainability is a stated priority of the Government of Canada and the Canadian Forest Service (Canada Forest Accord 2003–2008). Canada is home to more than 10% of the earth's forest, and approximately 40% of Canada's total landmass (more than 400 million ha) is forested. From a socio-economic perspective, forestry is the largest industry in Canada, supporting 324 000 direct jobs and contributing over $28 billion (data for 2006) to our balance of trade (Natural Resources Canada 2007). Canada's forests also support a multibillion-dollar recreation and tourism industry. Further, Canada's forests make significant ecological contributions to global processes and values by filtering air and water, regenerating soils, preventing erosion, and conserving unique ecological resources and communities.

Objectives to sustain these competing economic, social/cultural, and ecological forest values on forest land are often in competition. The result is a shrinking operational land base for traditional forestry operations. Further, forest harvesting, fire, insects, and diseases (hereafter referred to as agents of change) interact both spatially and temporally to alter the landscape and influence the production and hence availability of these forest values. In addition, climate change will likely alter the individual and interacting effects of these agents of change (Drever et al. 2006).

From a sustainable development perspective, the task is to understand and model the interactions of these agents of change and to assess their impacts on forest values. Resolving these issues dictates that we adopt a holistic (or ecosystem-based management) approach because of the highly integrated nature of ecological (and socioeconomic) systems. Although early attempts to implement sustainable development policies were led by government and focused on the environment, balancing economic, social, and environmental objectives is now a societal expectation, and in many jurisdictions a legislative requirement.

To meet the challenge in implementing sustainable forest management, we developed an integrated risk analysis (IRA) framework within which the threats posed by multiple (interacting) biotic and abiotic agents of change can be examined, and their potential impacts on multiple forest values (user-defined) evaluated in a holistic approach. Practically, our IRA framework is a simple (intuitive) framework of components that attempts to 1) characterize the attributes of any given landscape (for example, watershed, forest management district, ecoregion, province, etc.); 2) predict (model) future forest conditions under various scenarios; 3) model the potential impact of these scenarios on various economic, social, and ecological values; and 4) integratively assess the effects of the predicted future forest conditions on multiple forest values. In the remainder of this paper, we describe in more detail our concept of an IRA framework and provide an example currently being developed for the western region of the island portion of Newfoundland and Labrador.

INTEGRATED RISK ANALYSIS FRAMEWORK DESCRIPTION

Our IRA framework has four main components underlain with a common geospatial structure (Figure 1). Component 1 (**Agents of Change**) models various

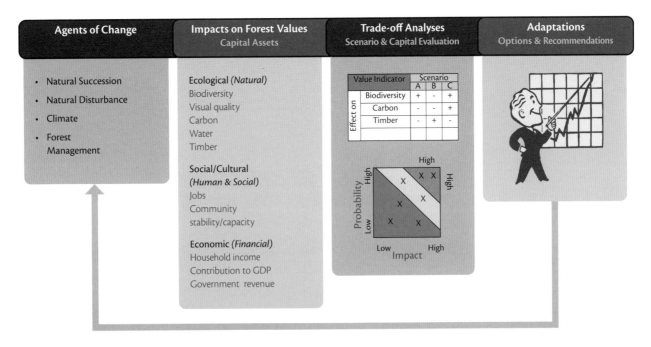

Agents of Change	Impacts on Forest Values Capital Assets	Trade-off Analyses Scenario & Capital Evaluation	Adaptations Options & Recommendations

Figure 1. Conceptual integrated risk analysis framework.

change agents to predict future landscapes that may result from a natural succession/natural disturbance regime, climate change, or as the product of a proposed forest management plan. Component 2 of the IRA framework (**Impacts on Forest Values**) individually models the impacts of any proposed future landscape on various forest values. These forest values of concern can be ecological or natural capital (for example, habitat for species of concern, rare forest types, timber volumes), social/cultural (human and social capital, for example, jobs, community stability), or economic (financial capital, for example, household income, contribution to the gross domestic product, government revenue); values modeled are inherently those that are valued ecosystem components for the spatial area of interest (that is, user-defined). Component 3 (**Trade-off Analyses**) conducts an integrated risk analysis (risk estimation, risk assessment, and risk management) to simultaneously evaluate the relative effects of various agents of change (including forest management) on economic, social, and ecological forest values on a common land base expressed in a common currency or with a common metric. This currency may be expressed very simply, for example, percentage change in forest value from current (baseline) conditions, or in a much more complex fashion, for example, expressing all outputs in monetary values, and would likely vary depending on the questions being asked, the complexity of the forest value models, data availability, etc. Component

4 (**Adaptations**) of our IRA framework assesses the outcomes of our trade-off analyses relative to targets or objectives and makes recommendations based on that assessment. For example, an IRA assessment of a proposed forest management plan may be illustrated as in Figure 2 in which a future forest landscape is simulated; the effects on various forest values assessed and quantified; risks quantitatively evaluated and assessed as to their acceptability; and plans implemented if the outcomes are acceptable, or modified in an interactive assessment loop if judged unacceptable. Finally, underlying these four major IRA components is a significant project activity centered on remote sensing and geospatial data development supporting the modeling of agents of change and forest values and application of models to a common land base (Luther et al. 2007).

INTEGRATED RISK ANALYSIS FRAMEWORK APPLICATION IN WESTERN NEWFOUNDLAND

We are currently applying our IRA framework to assess the impacts of proposed forest harvesting plans for a forest management district in western Newfoundland. This forest management district (District 15) is centered on a pulp and paper mill that is essential to the economic livelihood of many individuals and communities in the greater area. Some of the critical issues surrounding management of forest land in this district are 1) maintenance of a sustainable timber supply for the mill, and

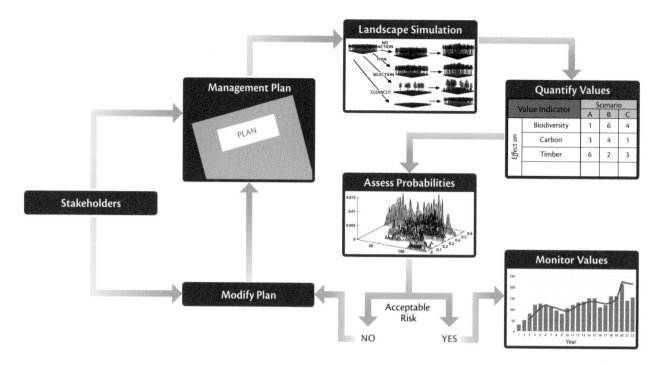

Figure 2. Implementation of the integrated risk analysis framework for a proposed forest management plan.

the direct and indirect economic benefits to the region; 2) protection of habitat for the federally and provincially listed endangered Newfoundland marten (*Martes americana atrata*), a small forest-dependent carnivore (Forsey et al.1995; Hearn 2007); 3) public perspective on viewscapes produced via forest harvesting (almost entirely clearcut logging); 4) protection of productive forests from insect defoliation, particularly defoliation outbreaks of hemlock looper (*Lambdina fiscellaria fiscellaria*); and 5) carbon sequestration consequences for proposed forest practices. Our interdisciplinary team consists of entomologists, wildlife ecologists, economists, remote sensing scientists, and climate change scientists, spread across federal and provincial government departments, forest industry, and academia. However, although the IRA team draws on the individual efforts of these science professionals, collectively the IRA framework approach delivers a synergistic "value-added" product from these individual science programs. Further, it is this collective effort that we believe will be closest to providing the science-based or best-available-information approach for policy decisions in support of multicriteria decision-making and ecosystem-based management planning.

Ultimately, the goal of the IRA framework described previously and its implementation in western Newfoundland is to support sustainable forest management and the development of effective forest management policy. Our IRA framework can be used at a variety of spatial and temporal scales to focus on local, regional, and national interests. Moreover, an IRA framework provides resource managers and policy makers with a tool to deal with the complex and interacting issues inherent in managing Canada's forests—a science-based tool to bridge the gap between science and policy.

ACKNOWLEDGMENTS

The integrated risk framework concept in general and the development of an integrated risk analysis framework for western Newfoundland in particular have been a collaborative effort of many individuals representing various provincial and federal government departments and several university and academic institutions. We thank all members of the CFS–IRA team and all individuals from partner organizations affiliated with the IRA project being implemented in western Newfoundland.

REFERENCES

Drever, C.R.; Peterson, G.; Messier, C.; Bergeron, Y.; Flannigan, M. 2006. Can forest management based on natural disturbances maintain ecological resilience? Can. J. For. Res. 36:2285–2299.

Forsey, O.; Bissonette, J.; Brazil, J.; Curnew, K.; Lemon, J.; Mayo, L.; Thompson, I.; Bateman, L.; O'Driscoll, L. 1995. National recovery plan for Newfoundland marten. Report No. 14, Recovery of Nationally Endangered Wildlife Committee, Ottawa, ON. 31 p.

Hearn, B. J. 2007. Factors affecting habitat selection and population characteristics of American marten (*Martes americana atrata*) in Newfoundland. Ph.D. thesis, University of Maine, Orono, ME.

Luther, J. E.; Fournier, R.A.; Hearn, B.J.; Piercey, D.; Royer, L.; Strickland, G. 2007. Remote sensing within an ecosystem-based management framework for sustainable forests. *In* Proceedings of ForestSat 2007: Forests and Remote Sensing: Methods and Operational Tools, 5–7 November 2007, Montpellier, France. http://forestsat.teledetection.fr [Accessed January 2008.]

Natural Resources Canada. 2007. The State of Canada's Forests. Annual Report 2007. Canadian Forest Service, Ottawa, ON. 28 p. http://canadaforests.nrcan.gc.ca/rpt#sustainable [Accessed January 2008.]

Socioeconomic Approaches to Integrated Land Management Decisions in the Foothills Model Forest and Beyond

Mike N. Patriquin Forest Economist, Northern Forestry Centre
Canadian Forest Service, Natural Resources Canada, Edmonton, AB

W.L. (Vic) Adamowicz Professor, Department of Rural Economy
University of Alberta, Edmonton, AB

INTRODUCTION

The Foothills Model Forest is a prime example of a regional landscape in Canada that because of its many competing interests requires innovative approaches to deal with complex resource management trade-offs. It encompasses a forested land base of over 2.75 million ha in west-central Alberta; is the second largest component of Canada's Model Forest Network (www.fmf.ab.ca); and comprises the forest management area of West Fraser Mills Ltd., several Crown management areas, and a variety of protected areas including Jasper National Park (Patriquin et al. 2007a). Forestry, oil and gas extraction, coal mining, and tourism are the major economic drivers operating on the landscape. Research in the region is, in part, focused on local-level indicators of sustainable forest management and the socioeconomic aspects of natural resource management (Foothills Model Forest 2000).

In this article, we describe two approaches that are being used in the Foothills Model Forest to investigate the economic consequences of alternative natural resource management policies on the area. The first approach is an economic simulation model to quantify the market economic consequences linked to biophysical or policy changes in the region. The second approach is natural resource accounting that values the stock and flow of natural resources and environmental services in the region according to a common dollar currency. The general intent of each approach is to gain an understanding of the benefits derived from a regional landscape for the purpose of more integrated and sustainable land management. We then discuss "choice experiments," a mechanism for informing land management decisions through the elicitation of public preferences for trade-offs associated with a variety of land management policies.

LINKED BIOPHYSICAL AND ECONOMIC SIMULATION APPROACH

The general framework for this approach is simulation of the economic consequences of biophysical changes on natural resource availability using an economic impact model. For example, under this framework, a resource manager would have access to a suite of biophysical indicators; the supply of market-oriented resources (such as the timber supply) could then be used as an input to the economic impact model to investigate the economic consequences of alternative land management policies on resource supply.

General equilibrium models are standard tools for examining the effects of policy changes or economic shocks on employment and income (Alavalapati et al. 1996). In common practice, these models are used to simulate economic conditions with and without the change on an economy-wide basis. One of the first innovations to economic approaches in the Foothills Model Forest was the development of a regional computable general equilibrium (CGE) framework that relaxed some of the extensively criticized assumptions in the more widely used, but far less flexible, input–output models (Patriquin et al. 2003b).

The Foothills Model Forest went through a process of developing a suite of local-level indicators of sustainable forest management that includes a variety of biophysical, economic, and social indicators. Tracking these indicators allows land managers to gauge the relative success of resource management policies (Foothills Model Forest 2000). In addition to this process, the regional CGE model developed for the Foothills Model Forest was used to investigate a variety of real and hypothetical changes to the regional economy in the context of natural resource management linked to changes in biophysical indicators. For example, a CGE model was recently used to simulate the employment and income impacts of timber-supply changes resulting from a hypothetical mountain pine beetle (*Dendroctonus ponderosae*) infestation in the region (Phillips et al. 2007).

The economic impact modeling, linked to biophysical indicators, can be used to assess the relative benefits of alternative land management policies, but this framework does not use a common currency and places the onus on the land manager to judge the relative importance of trade-offs among the biophysical and economic variables. The benefit of this framework is that it provides land managers with a large amount of information on the response of a suite of indicators under various management alternatives. The challenge with this framework is the lack of a clear mechanism for the land manager to judge a preferred set of management policies based both on science and on societal preferences.

This general framework for integrating social and biological information in land management decisions has been widely applied on a case study basis on regional landscapes within western Canada. For example, a linked biophysical economic simulation process was applied in the Robson Valley Enhanced Forest Management Pilot Program, the Morice and Lakes Innovative Forest Practices Agreement, the Government of Canada's Mountain Pine Beetle Initiative, and the Northeast Slopes Integrated Resource Management Pilot Program (Moon et al. 2004; ML IFPA 2004; Patriquin et al. 2005; Patriquin et al. 2007b; NES Regional Steering Group 2003).

NATURAL RESOURCE ACCOUNTING

The second approach, natural resource accounting, involves applying a value (in a common dollar currency) to all of the net benefits flowing off a landscape. This includes both market benefits through the extraction and development of natural resources and non-market benefits such as the provision of ecosystem services. Valuing the stock and flow of services generated through

natural capital allows the assessment of the potential impact of resource use on human welfare now and for future generations (Patriquin et al. 2004).

Natural resource accounts provide a more complete indication of well-being compared with conventional economic accounts through consistent treatment of all forms of capital and through an indicator of the net benefits resulting from economic activity. As a tool for integrated land management (ILM), natural resource accounting provides a framework for organizing biophysical and economic indicators, and through valuation techniques it may also help set realistic prices for public assets (for example, royalty rates) (Haener and Adamowicz 2000).

The natural resource account developed for the Foothills Model Forest considers both market activities (that is, forestry, subsurface minerals, tourism, trapping, fishing, and the rest of the economy) and non-market activities (that is, recreational hunting, fishing, and camping, subsistence use, passive use, biodiversity maintenance, and environmental control service such as carbon sequestration) (Patriquin et al. 2004). For example, in the Foothills Model Forest, the total net benefit (in 1996 dollars) derived from market activities was about $508 million and from non-market activities, about $107 million (Patriquin et al. 2004). Tracking how these values change through time may provide an indication of changes in the sustainability of the region.

The challenges in developing and using natural resource accounts in ecosystem approaches and ILM are threefold. First, resource accounting on a regional basis is constrained by the ability to obtain data and appropriately value the necessary components (that is, including the public acceptance of placing a monetary value on ecosystem services). Second, there does not appear to be a general consensus on the approaches and the valuation techniques employed. Third, natural resource accounts are a snapshot of current or historical conditions and by themselves are not models and do not simulate future indicator levels.

Although many of these challenges remain, progress is being made. For example, there are now two examples of regional natural resource accounts in Alberta (Haener and Adamowicz 2000; Patriquin et al. 2004). There is also an example from the Foothills Model Forest of an economic impact model that incorporates linkages to natural capital through a simple resource account to simulate changes in market and non-market activities in response to policy changes (Patriquin et al. 2003a).

Unlike the biophysical indicators linked to a simulation model, the largest benefit of using a natural resource accounting framework is that it yields a suite of indicators with a common monetary metric. Arguably, this would allow resource managers to find balance and make trade-off decisions among a more directly comparable set of indicators.

Although both of the approaches mentioned above are based on sound science, neither of them necessarily involve a clear mechanism for incorporating public preferences in the land management decision beyond broad democratic processes. Choice experiments may provide a way to incorporate public preferences into decision making. Choice experiments are not only a useful tool for identifying the monetary value of non-market components within a natural resource account, but they can also provide land managers with support for publicly preferred management options in ILM or ecosystem-based management processes.

CHOICE EXPERIMENTS: A MECHANISM FOR SCIENCE-BASED, PUBLICLY PREFERRED MANAGEMENT DECISIONS

Stated preference methods, such as choice experiments, are used to derive the value of non-market benefits by using individuals' stated behavior in hypothetical situations (Bateman et al. 2002; Louviere 2001; Bennett and Adamowicz 2001; Alpizar et al. 2001). In a choice experiment, individual respondents are asked to choose their preferred alternative among several different alternatives across a sequence of choice sets. Each alternative is described by select attributes and levels, including a monetary value. When individuals make their choices, they implicitly make trade-offs between the levels of attributes in the choice set.

Choice experiments are a potential mechanism that resource managers could apply in an integrated land management framework. Choice experiments, or similar preference elicitation mechanisms, can provide information on trade-offs that members of the public are willing to make. Given a description of trade-offs that arise from different land use management strategies,

choice experiments can provide information on those strategies most preferred by the public.

In principle, choice experiments could provide information on trade-offs between efficiency issues (that is, the size of market or non-market benefits generating in a scenario) and equity issues (that is, who benefits and who does not benefit). Choice experiments can also help understand trade-offs that are not reflected in current economic or ecological conditions. Choice experiments are not free from challenges and criticism (Bennett and Blamey 2001). For example, although choice experiments can provide information on public preferences, it is quite challenging to incorporate dynamics into such preference elicitation, limiting the types of preferences that can be elicited. Choice experiments also suffer from the fact that as stated preference mechanisms they are based on expressed preferences rather than values based on actual transactions or actual political processes.

CONCLUSION

General equilibrium modeling provides information on economic impacts, while resource accounts are intended to provide information on welfare effects (economic efficiency). The studies from the Foothills Model Forest provide examples of these techniques and how they can provide insight into economic consequences of alternative actions (policies, etc). They can also be linked to give more complete descriptions of impacts and to a certain extent they can provide insights into equity as well as efficiency impacts. Although these techniques have been applied in a variety of regional land management initiatives in western Canada, an element that appears to be lacking is a rigorous mechanism for evaluating publicly preferred management alternatives.

Based on our experiences in the Foothills Model Forest, we believe that choice experiments have a role in integrated land management frameworks within an ecosystem approach. They can provide information on overarching issues, such as trade-offs between the equity and efficiency of different outcomes, or trade-offs between elements that can be monetized and measured in commensurable ways, and those that cannot. This might be quite useful to decision makers since the political process may be too broad to capture preferences for individual regional land management issues. Choice experiments may have advantages and disadvantages relative to other mechanisms for eliciting public preferences (for example, polls, deliberative processes, etc.), but also offer the potential for unique economic insights regarding trade-offs, beyond those obtainable through general equilibrium modeling and natural resource accounting.

REFERENCES

Alavalapati, J.; White, W.; Jagger, P.; Wellstead, A. 1996. Effect of land use restrictions on the economy of Alberta: a computable general equilibrium analysis. Can. J. Reg. Sci. 19:349–365.

Alpizar, F.; Carlsson, F.; Martinsson, P. 2001. Using choice experiments for non-market valuation. Göteborg University, Department of Economics, Göteborg, Sweden. Working Papers in Economics No. 52.

Bateman, I.J.; Carson, R.T.; Day, B.; Hanemann, M.; Hanley, N.; Hett, T.; Jones-Lee, M.; Loomes, G.; Mourato, S.; Özdemiroglu, E.; Pearce, D.; Sugden, R.; Swanson, J. 2002. Economic valuation with stated preference techniques: a manual. Edward Elgar, Cheltenham, UK. 480 p.

Bennett, J.; Adamowicz, W. 2001. Some fundamentals of environmental choice modeling. Pages 37–72 in J.Bennett and R. Blamey (eds.). The choice modelling approach to environmental valuation. Edward Elgar, Cheltenham, UK. 269 p.

Bennett, J.; Blamey, R. 2001. The strengths and weaknesses of environmental choice modeling. Pages 227–242 in J. Bennett and R. Blamey (eds.). The choice modelling approach to environmental valuation. Edward Elgar, Cheltenham, UK. 269 p.

Foothills Model Forest. 2000. Local level indicators of sustainable forest management for the Foothills Model Forest: initial status report. Foothills Model Forest, Hinton, AB.

Haener, M.; Adamowicz, W. 2000. Regional forest resource accounting: a northern Alberta case study. Can J. For. Res. 30:264–273.

Louviere, J.J. 2001. Choice experiments: an overview of concepts and issues. Pages 13–36 in J. Bennett and R. Blamey (eds.). The choice modelling approach to environmental valuation. Edward Elgar, Cheltenham, UK. 269 p.

[ML IFPA] Morice and Lakes Innovative Forest Practices Agreement. 2004. Project summary: economic impact modeling in the Morice & Lakes IFPA region. Summary No. 43, June 2004.

Moon, A.; Patriquin, M.; White, W.; Spence, M. 2004. Economic overview of the Robson Valley Forest District. BC J. Ecosys. Manag. 4(2):1–20.

NES [Northern East Slopes] Regional Steering Group. 2003. Recommendations to the Minister of the Environment for: the northern east slopes sustainable resource and environmental management strategy. Alberta Environment, Edmonton, AB.

Patriquin, M.; Alavalapati, J.; Adamowicz, W.; White, W. 2003a. Incorporating natural capital into economy-wide impact analysis: a case study from Alberta. Environ. Monit. Assess. 86:149–169.

Patriquin, M.; Alavalapati, J.; Wellstead, A.; Young, S.; Adamowicz, W.; White, W. 2003b. Estimating impacts of resource management policies in the Foothills Model Forest. Can. J. For. Res. 33:147–155.

Patriquin, M.; Heckbert, S.; Nickerson, C.; Spence, M.; White, W. 2005. Regional economic implications of the mountain pine beetle infestation in the Northern Interior Forest Region of British Columbia. Natural Resources Canada, Canadian Forest Service, Pacific Forestry Centre, Victoria, BC. Mountain Pine Beetle Initiative Working Paper 2005-3.

Patriquin, M.; Lantz, V.; Furtas, R.; Ambard, M.; White, W. 2007a. Socioeconomic transition in the Foothills Model Forest from 1996 to 2001. Natural Resources Canada, Canadian Forest Service, Northern Forestry Centre, Edmonton, AB/Foothills Model Forest, Hinton, AB. Inf. Rep. NOR-X-410.

Patriquin, M.; Spence, M.; White, W. 2004. Accounting for natural resources in the Foothills Model Forest. Natural Resources Canada, Canadian Forest Service, Northern Forestry Centre, Edmonton, AB/Foothills Model Forest, Hinton, AB. Inf. Rep. NOR-X-398.

Patriquin, M.; Wellstead, A.; White, W. 2007b. Beetles, trees, and people: regional economic impact sensitivity and policy considerations related to the mountain pine beetle infestation in British Columbia, Canada. For. Policy Econ. 9:938–946.

Phillips, B.; Beck, J.; Nickel, T. 2007. Managing the economic impacts of mountain pine beetle outbreaks in Alberta: Foothills Model Forest case study. University of Alberta, Edmonton, AB. Western Centre for Economic Research Inf. Bull. No. 100.

Recent Efforts, Experiments, and Lessons Learned

Sustainable Resource and Environmental Management in Alberta

Morris Seiferling Assistant Deputy Minister
Sustainable Resource and Environmental Management
Alberta Government, Edmonton, AB

INTRODUCTION

In the past, Alberta's economic prosperity was based on the development and use of its abundant natural resources. However, driven by recent extraordinary levels of energy development and the pressure this has created on our land and water use, infrastructure, labor, housing, and society, there is a growing expectation that the manner in which these resources will be developed must change.

Societal values are changing, particularly in relation to natural resource development and the environment. Environmental protection is being viewed increasingly as a societal value as the effects of economic growth on climate, air quality, water use, biodiversity, and land use are recognized.

With this in mind, there are several significant challenges/opportunities facing Alberta:

- The energy sector is expected to continue to expand, driven by strong markets, enhanced recovery of conventional oil and gas, development of large unconventional resources like oil sands and coal bed methane, new renewable resources such as biofuels and increased value-added processing.

- Population growth and urbanization is expected to continue, fueled by economic prosperity and an enviable quality of life.

- Population, urban, and industrial growth are resulting in air and water quality challenges. Competing uses for airshed capacity need to be managed in conjunction with point and non-point air emissions management.

- Rapid growth, climate change, and uses of water and watersheds are causing Albertans to look at the way we manage our water and aquatic ecosystems.

- Natural ecosystems are under increasing pressures from climate variability, habitat loss, and increasing numbers of invasive plant and animal species.

- There is a growing desire for the better coordination between decisions on subsurface and surface decisions for resource development and a growing concern among resource industries about timely and appropriate access to the land and about their *social license* or public support to operate.

These issues are not discrete and can no longer be dealt with separately. As such, consideration of environmental matters and shared outcomes of air quality, water quality and quantity, biodiversity, and expectations regarding the development of the provincial land base—both surface and subsurface—becomes very complex indeed.

THE RESPONSE

In response, the Government of Alberta has committed to the Sustainable Resource and Environmental Management (SREM) of the province's natural resources by

1. considering and integrating the associated economic, environmental, and social implications into decision making;

2. fulfilling expectations as they relate to the needs of future generations—that is, adopting a long-term perspective on the use of natural resources, both non-renewable and renewable, to ensure their long-term viability and future use potential; and

3. fulfilling the commitment of maintaining a sustainable environment.

The departments of Energy, Environment, and Sustainable Resource Development, in particular, have committed to developing shared natural resource and environmental outcomes and strengthening their collective business approaches and partnerships.

A Strategic Systems Approach

A key component of SREM is the use of a strategic systems approach (Figure 1) driven by clear, concrete resource and environmental outcomes and performance measures. This approach relies on a sound understanding of our natural resources and the environment (for example, watersheds, airsheds, ecosystems) and an effective management system where the achievement of outcomes is supported by integrated policies across government, effective delivery of programs and services, open and transparent performance assessment, and on-going adaptation for improvement. It is supported by shared information systems.

The systems approach is also based on collaboration among government departments, other levels of governments, industry, non-governmental organizations, academic–scientific–technical communities, other stakeholders, and the public. Effective collaboration requires clearly defined roles and responsibilities for achieving the outcomes.

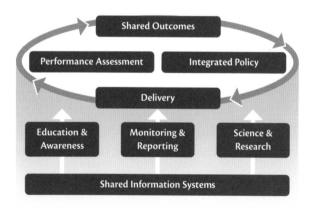

Figure 1. Alberta's strategic systems approach.

A brief description of the key elements of the strategic systems approach follows:

- **Shared outcomes.** Refers to the desired/expected endpoint or state developed and defined using a collaborative approach.

- **Performance assessment.** Refers to the process of comparing and analyzing current conditions and trends to create knowledge on the performance in achieving natural resource and environmental outcomes. The performance of these actions is then measured against the outcomes in an on-going cycle for continuous improvement.

- **Integrated policy.** The process of aligning/coordinating policies from a range of interests and expectations.

- **Delivery.** Refers to the processes, programs, and services undertaken to implement policies and achieve outcomes. Delivery can be accomplished through both regulatory and non-regulatory approaches.

- **Shared information systems.** Involve activities such as monitoring and reporting, science and research, and education and awareness.

The strategic systems approach is supported and made possible by the following principles:

- **Resource and environmental stewardship.** Stewardship is a principle or approach whereby citizens, industry, communities, and governments work together as stewards of the province's natural resources and environment. In general terms, stewardship means managing one's life, property, resources, and environment with regard for the rights or interests of others.

- **Government-wide vision and goals.** Government-wide outcomes, policies, and strategies will be the basis for shared implementation of resource and environmental management. As appropriate, there will be integrated policy development, business plans, budgets, and performance measures.

- **Shared responsibility.** Shared responsibility recognizes that resource and environmental management is not solely the responsibility of government. It is based on cooperation, collaboration, and partnerships among parties that have an interest in achieving resource and environmental outcomes.

- **Flexible regulatory and non-regulatory tools.** This principle recognizes the need for a set of flexible compliance assurance tools and incentives made up of a combination of both regulatory and non-regulatory instruments. Non-regulatory instruments involve performance-based systems that promote performance beyond compliance. The driving mechanism is financial incentives and stewardship.

- **Continuous improvement.** Continuous improvement is based on the need to continuously monitor performance and success and to strive for improvement. The goal is on-going improvement in achieving environmental and resource outcomes, as well as improvements in the management systems used to achieve the outcomes.

NATURAL RESOURCE DEVELOPMENT WITHIN A NEW MANAGEMENT MODEL

The challenges faced by Alberta and the need for a strategic systems approach to sustainable development and environmental management have led to the recognition that a new management model is required. In this context, the role of government is one of managing and/or making possible natural resource development for the economic prosperity of the province.

In the past, we managed this process as a series of discrete activities through "command and control" mechanisms; that is, we established "rules" related to particular development projects, activities, events, and/or environmental mediums; measured compliance with those rules; and intervened when the rules were broken.

This model was premised on several assumptions, but central was the assumption of abundance. We assumed that we had plenty of air, water, and land, and if some event happened to compromise any one of them, we simply had to stop doing whatever it was we were doing and everything would be fine. More importantly, the assumption was that as long as everyone complied with the rules, everything would be fine. Further, we operated under the premise that events affecting one medium or another were manageable as independent interests—air, water, land, and even biodiversity were separable mediums that could be managed discretely.

Increasingly, we find scarcity in things we once thought were abundant; we find that just stopping an activity is either not an option or does not solve the problem; we find that everyone simply following the rules does not consider the cumulative effects of the collective activities; and we find that air, water, land, and consequently biodiversity are inseparably linked. Ultimately, we find that we need a new model.

First we must consider several key issues:

- Recognize and manage the overall cumulative effects of development at various geographical levels and across all environmental mediums (air, land, water, and biodiversity);

- Guide the making of development decisions within clearly defined expected outcomes;

- Explicitly recognize the inseparable nature of the environmental mediums; and

- Manage sustainable resources and environmental outcomes as a single system through legislative framework(s).

Natural resource development remains central in this new model (Figure 2), but accomplished within the parameters of acceptable environmental outcomes related not only to individual projects but also the cumulative effects of development. The expectation remains that development of the natural resources themselves is undertaken primarily by private interests within a free-market economy. Certain economic and social outcomes are tied directly to development based on the social benefits derived from these activities.

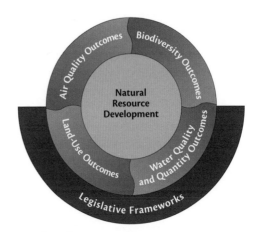

Figure 2. Alberta's new natural resources management model.

Government has a significant role within this core (that is, policy frameworks, regulation, taxation, royalties, and mineral/surface rights disposition), but the major function is that of assurance of the public interest. The system is held together by the legislative frameworks that enable the systems to set targets and monitor and hold participants, both individually and collectively, accountable and become the mechanism or management instruments for defining and achieving acceptable developmental targets. Planning within this context, therefore, involves understanding the dynamics of the core activity—natural resource development—and then defining the strategic challenges related to the environmental parameters and managing to the desired and agreed upon outcomes.

The Suite of Strategies

The Government of Alberta is developing a suite of integrated strategies to focus on growth pressures related to natural resources and the environment. They are components of a broader commitment to consider the resource and environmental sustainability challenges of today, tomorrow, and the future.

The strategies are created at several scales and focus points to consider fundamental components of environmental or natural resource management from strategic visioning to on-the-ground operations. When complete, the strategies will be robust enough to respond to changing trends and issues over time.

How Do Things Fit Together?

We need to look at the many interconnections between these strategies (Figure 3). Alberta is currently developing or reviewing several broad, overarching strategies that will give policy direction to managing its land and natural resources into the future. It is also developing operational policies/programs (which apply province-wide but are more specific in their direction). Finally, Alberta is looking at developing and amending legislation to support this environment and natural resource management regulatory framework to enable sustainable development by considering the cumulative effects of development on land, air, water, and biodiversity.

Figure 3. Linkages between Alberta's environment and natural resources management strategies.

Land-Use Framework

The Land-Use Framework will provide an approach to better manage public and private lands and natural resources to meet Alberta's long-term economic, social, and environmental goals. It will provide the overarching government direction and guidance to help balance the various demands on our land and natural resources.

Water for Life Strategy

The strategy focuses on Alberta's long-term water quality and water quantity challenges.

Climate Change Plan

The Climate Change Plan will help focus on Alberta's responsibility for reducing greenhouse gases.

Biodiversity Strategy

The strategy will provide the context and guidance for biodiversity conservation in Alberta as a component of the implementation of the Land-Use Framework.

Wetlands Policy

The policy will help focus on the loss of wetlands in Alberta as a component of the implementation of the Water for Life Strategy.

Cumulative effects

A new cumulative effects management framework will help focus on the regional cumulative effects on the environment from development based on established environmental objectives. A pilot project is currently underway north of Edmonton.

Integrated Land Management Program

The program is focused on reducing the footprint of industrial, commercial, and recreational use of public land while ensuring an appropriate level of access to develop resources.

Upstream Oil and Gas Integration Project

The project is developing an integrated policy framework and delivery system that will provide a consistent approach to managing upstream oil and gas development activities, with clear and consistent information and expectations for government, industry, and the public.

Ecosystem-based Management in the Central and North Coast Areas of British Columbia

Andy MacKinnon Research Ecologist, Coast Region
British Columbia Ministry of Forests and Range, Victoria, BC

INTRODUCTION

In the mid-1990s, the British Columbia government put in place a system of multiparty land-use planning for 23 large regions throughout the province. The process is referred to as Land and Resource Management Planning (LRMP). In this article, I will discuss two of the LRMP areas that form part of coastal British Columbia, the Central Coast and the North Coast.

The Central Coast LRMP area—also known as the Great Bear Rainforest—covers 4.6 million ha and the North Coast LRMP area, 1.0 million ha, along the mainland coast. Together they include the largest areas of undeveloped coastal temperate rainforest in the world (Ecotrust, Pacific GIS, and Conservation International 1995; MacKinnon 2003). Lower elevations here are characterized by near continuous coniferous forests featuring western redcedar (*Thuja plicata*) and western hemlock (*Tsuga heterophylla*), along with amabilis fir (*Abies amabilis*), Sitka spruce (*Picea sitchensis*), and Douglas-fir (*Pseudotsuga menziesii*) in the south. Outer coast ecosystems are often bogs or bog forests, with shore pine (*Pinus contorta* var. *contorta*) and yellow-cedar (*Chamaecyparis nootkatensis*). Subalpine areas feature more mountain hemlock (*Tsuga mertensiana*) and yellow-cedar, and alpine areas occur above 1200 m in the south and 800 m in the north. These forests are home to some of the world's most viable populations of grizzly (brown) bears, wolves, five species of salmon, and more. As well as attracting much international attention, the Central and North Coast areas are greatly valued by the environmental community, by forest companies, and especially by the people who live there.

First Nations, industry, environmental groups, local governments, and other stakeholders collaborated during the LRMP process to establish a planning table for each area. The provincial government used the planning table reports as position papers in negotiations with many First Nations in the Central and North Coast areas. These government-to-government (First Nations to provincial) negotiations resulted in the land-use plans in place there today.[1] The plans set aside 28% of the land base as protected areas. Over the rest of the land base, the mandate is to practice "ecosystem-based management."

LAYING THE GROUNDWORK

Part of the process of planning for the Central and North Coast LRMP areas was the establishment of the Coast Information Team, a non-government panel of experts in social, economic, and biological research. This team prepared materials in support of the planning process, including the report *Ecosystem-based Management Planning Handbook*.[2] It provides the basis for ecosystem-based management in the Central and North Coast areas.

The handbook defines ecosystem-based management as "an adaptive approach to managing human activities that seeks to ensure the coexistence of healthy, fully functioning ecosystems and human communities. The intent is to maintain those spatial and temporal

---

[1] Documentation on the coast land-use decision implementation can be found at www.ilmbwww.gov.bc.ca/lup/lrmp/coast/central_north_coast/index.html.

[2] A copy of this report can be found at http://ilmbwww.gov.bc.ca/citbc.

characteristics of ecosystems such that component species and ecological processes can be sustained, and human well-being supported and improved." Ecosystem-based management is based on the following principles:

- Maintenance of ecological integrity.

- Respect for the rights, title, and interests of Aboriginal peoples.

- Promotion of human well-being.

- Sustainability of cultures, communities, and economies within the context of healthy ecosystems.

- Application of the precautionary principle.

- Collaboration in planning and management.

- Fair distribution of land-use and resource benefits.

These principles drive two goals and their associated objectives:

Goals	Objectives
Maintain the ecological integrity of terrestrial, marine, and freshwater ecosystems	· Maintain ecosystem functions and processes (for example, streamflow, water quality, soil productivity, natural disturbance rates and patterns) across scales and through the long term.
	· Maintain the natural diversity of species, genes, and habitat elements across scales and over time.
	· Protect and where necessary restore underrepresented, endangered, or degraded ecosystems.
Achieve high levels of human well-being	· Recognize and accommodate Aboriginal rights, title, and interests in the land and its resources.
	· Achieve the health, wealth, and educational status required for a high-quality and secure life for Aboriginal and non-Aboriginal peoples.
	· Build stable, resilient, well-serviced, and peaceful communities in coastal British Columbia.
	· Create a strong, diverse economy and mix of businesses in communities and across the region.
	· Create a strong and diverse mix of non-profit and voluntary organizations and a vibrant set of traditional, cultural, and non-market activities within communities and across the region.
	· Ensure a fair distribution of benefits, costs, and risks to Aboriginal and non-Aboriginal peoples across all parts of coastal British Columbia

IMPLEMENTING ECOSYSTEM-BASED MANAGEMENT

Many more biologists than social scientists and economists were involved in the development of the ecosystem-based management approach for the North and Central Coast LRMP areas (Figure 1). As a result, the *Ecosystem-based Management Planning Handbook* is primarily directed towards the first goal: maintaining the ecological integrity of the areas. Little guidance on how to achieve high levels of human well-being (the second goal) is presented. I will therefore confine the rest of this article to a discussion of the first goal. However, I and others agree that successful implementation of an ecosystem-based management approach depends on meeting both goals and that it is unlikely that the first goal can be achieved without meeting the second one.

The key to meeting the first goal for ecosystem-based management is planning. For the LRMP areas, planning takes place at multiple scales and through collaborative efforts:

Scale	Land base (ha)	Example of collaborative effort
Regional	10 million +	Regional agreements and policies
Territory/ sub-regional	500 000 – 5 million	Strategic land-use plans
Landscape	30 000–100 000	Landscape reserves
Watershed	1 000–50 000	Resource-use and development plans
Site	<250	Business and project plans

Much of the planning is associated with risk management. For ecological integrity, it is assumed that the further systems are from a "natural" (that is, unmanaged) state, the greater the risk to ecological integrity. Deviations from the range of natural variability (RONV) are classed into risk classes: for example, a less than 30% deviation is low risk and a greater than 70% deviation is high risk. These figures (30% and 70%) were chosen because some research has shown that habitat supply thresholds around 30% and 70% (see Dykstra 2004). I will use a very wet hypermaritime variant of coastal temperate rainforest (CWHvh2) to show how these figures and risk classes might be applied. Data gathered for the LRMP areas suggest an undisturbed landscape in this variant would have 85–93% old-growth forest (more than 250 years old). "Low risk" is then defined as a landscape having more than 70% of the naturally occurring old-growth forest (that is, 70% × [85–93%] = [60–65%]) and "high risk" as a landscape having less than 30% of the naturally occurring old-growth forest (that is 30% × [85–93%] = [26–28%]).

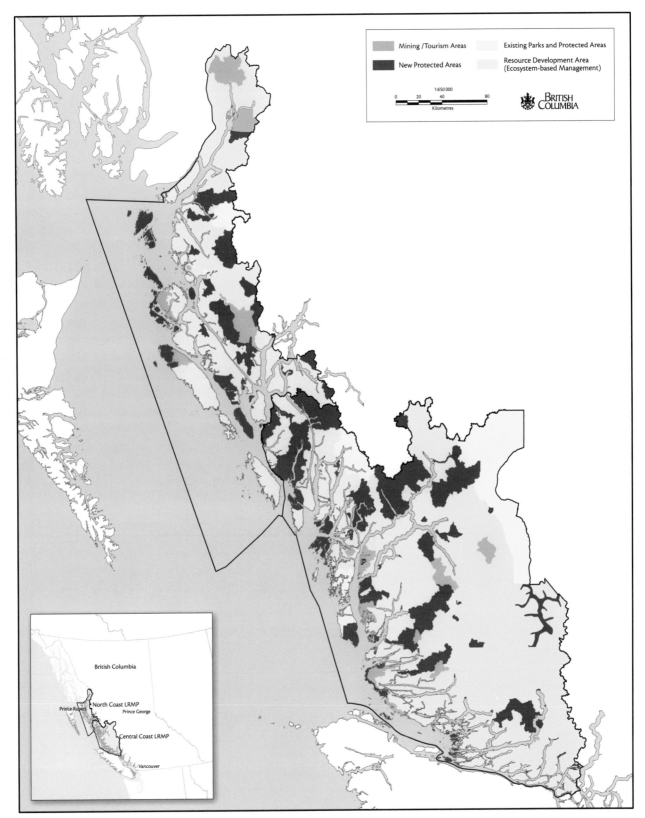

Figure 1. Central and North Coast Land and Resource Management and Planning (LRMP) areas, British Columbia.

Risk classes vary across the planning area. Overall, the planning area has to be managed with the objective of keeping the risk to ecological integrity low—in the above example, the CWHvh2 over millions of hectares would have to be at least 60–65% old-growth forest. But at landscape and watershed levels, level of risk could vary. For instance, some watersheds might be managed for moderate risk, and even a few for high risk, but none for less than the high risk threshold for old-growth forest (26–28%).

Management of the Central and North Coast LRMP areas to maintain ecological integrity includes the following:

- **Protect old-growth forests.** A certain percentage of naturally occurring old-growth forest must be maintained in each landscape and watershed unit; see example above.

- **Maintain forest structure at the stand level.** A minimum 15% of each area logged must be retained as individual trees or clumps of trees.

- **Protect threatened and endangered species and ecosystems.** Red-listed ecosystems (ecosystems designated most threatened in British Columbia according to categories described by NatureServe) and 50% of blue-listed ecosystems (the second most threatened class) must be retained.[3]

- **Protect wetlands.** Various wetland classes are specified for protection. For example, managers must maintain greater than 90% of the natural riparian forest next to estuaries and greater than 50% of the natural riparian forest next to fens and forested swamps. There is also the Coast Information Team's 2004 *Hydroriparian Planning Guide*,[4] to aid in implementing ecosystem-based management.

- **Apply adaptive management.** A fairly standard approach to practising adaptive management is specified. This recognizes that many of the assumptions underlying application of ecosystem-based management—on social, economic, and ecological grounds—are "best guesses" and require active testing and/or local calibration.

CONCLUDING REMARKS

The land-use plan for Haida Gwaii (Queen Charlotte Islands), off British Columbia's north coast, is just being developed, but will likely specify application of ecosystem-based management as well. I expect that ecosystem-based management will have a slightly different definition for Haida Gwaii: many of the same principles, but a different suite of practices. This seems appropriate for application in different ecosystems and in different social and economic circumstances.

Implementation of ecosystem-based management in British Columbia's central and north coast has just begun. I believe the most important challenge facing land managers here is not on the biological front, but on the social and economic one; that is, they need better ways of achieving high levels of human well-being (Goal 2). Even if that challenge is met, recommended approaches to simultaneously achieving the two goals—ecosystem integrity and human well-being—are only best guesses today. A program of adaptive management accompanying the implementation of ecosystem-based management is critical to the success of the process.

REFERENCES

Dykstra, P.R. 2004. Thresholds in habitat supply: a review of the literature. British Columbia Ministry of Sustainable Resource Management/Ministry of Water, Land and Air Protection, Victoria, BC. Wildlife Rep. R-27.

Ecotrust; Pacific GIS; Conservation International. 1995. The rain forests of home: an atlas of people and place. Part 1. Natural forests and native languages of the coastal temperate rain forest. Authors, Portland, OR. 24 p.

MacKinnon, A. 2003. West coast, temperate, old-growth forests. For. Chron. 79(3):475–484.

---

[3] More on British Columbia's red and blue lists of endangered species and ecosystems can be found at http://www.env.gov. bc.ca/atrisk/red-blue.htm.

[4] A copy of this report can be found at http://www.citbc.org/ ebmhydr.html.

Stand Level Adaptive Management (SLAM) Mixedwood Project

James A. Rice Research Forester, Ontario Forest Research Institute
Ontario Ministry of Natural Resources, Sault Ste Marie, ON

Rongzhou Man Research Scientist, Ontario Forest Research Institute
Ontario Ministry of Natural Resources, Sault Ste Marie, ON

INTRODUCTION

In this paper, we outline how the Stand Level Adaptive Management (SLAM) Mixedwood Project, an initiative of forest sector partners from industry, government, and non-profit organizations, provides a working model for the ecosystem approach to forest management in Ontario.

ECOSYSTEM APPROACH TO MANAGEMENT

The Convention on Biological Diversity and its Subsidiary Body on Scientific, Technical and Technological Advice (SBSTTA) have endorsed the use of an ecosystem approach for managing natural resources and maintaining biodiversity on the landscape (CBD 1995). The core of the Convention's definition (CBD 2000) states that an ecosystem approach

- "is a strategy for the integrated management of land, water and living resources that promotes conservation and sustainable use in an equitable way";

- "is based on the application of appropriate scientific methodologies focused on levels of biological organization, which encompass the essential structure, processes, functions and interactions among organisms and their environment";

- "requires adaptive management to deal with the complex and dynamic nature of ecosystems and the absence of complete knowledge or understanding of their functioning"; and

- "does not preclude other management and conservation approaches…but could, rather, integrate all these approaches and other methodologies to deal with complex situations."

In many ways, an ecosystem approach as described in the Convention is similar to the ecological sustainability approach that is prescribed in Ontario for natural resource management.

CONTEXT FOR FOREST MANAGEMENT IN ONTARIO

The Ontario Ministry of Natural Resources (OMNR) is responsible for the sustainable management of the province's vast and diverse range of natural resources.

Ontario has over 70.4 million ha of forested landscape of which about 24 million are classified as productive forests and managed for a full range of benefits. The Crown owns about 90% of the forested landscape and thus directs the management activities it allows on these lands (OMNR 2007).

As well, the province has over 3200 plant, 160 fish, 80 amphibian and reptile, 400 bird, and 85 mammal species. Most of these plants and animals live in or use the forests for food (OMNR 2007).

The OMNR has led the development of legislation, strategic documents, and policy directives to support the management of these resources. The key piece of legislation affecting forest management is the *Crown Forest Sustainability Act* (CFSA 1994), which states that

- "Large, healthy, diverse and productive Crown forests and their associated ecological processes and biological diversity should be conserved."

- "The long term health and vigour of Crown forests should be provided for by using forest practices that, within the limits of silvicultural requirements, emulate natural disturbances and landscape patterns while minimizing adverse effects on plant life, animal life, water, soil, air and social and economic values, including recreational values and heritage values."

OMNR's most-recent strategic directions are contained in *Our Sustainable Future* (OMNR 2005). It describes OMNR's vision—"a healthy environment that is naturally diverse and supports a high quality of life for the people of Ontario through sustainable development"—and mission—"to manage our natural resources in an ecologically sustainable way to ensure that they are available for the enjoyment and use of future generations."

Finally OMNR's policies, including the *Policy Framework for Sustainable Forests* (OMNR 1995), clearly identify that forest management must maintain ecological processes, biological diversity, and representative forested lands within a framework of ecological sustainability. The result is that any forest management activity recommended for use on Crown forests in Ontario must be ecologically appropriate and contribute to specific management objectives.

BOREAL MIXEDWOODS IN ONTARIO— AN OVERVIEW

Ontario has chosen to define boreal mixedwoods (BMW) in terms of the site and stand conditions they grow in (MacDonald 1995):

- A BMW **site** is a fertile upland site in the boreal forest region that favors productive mixtures of spruce, balsam fir, aspen, and white birch.

- A BMW **stand** is a forested stand on a BMW site where no single species exceeds 80% of the stand's basal area.

BMW stands are highly diverse ecosystems containing mixtures of tree species that offer diversity to the forest's vertical and horizontal structure. They have high biomass productivity potential and offer habitat diversity, pest resistance, and visual appeal (MacDonald 1995).

In the past, however, these stands were seldom managed to maintain a mixedwood composition. Deliberate

management for mixedwoods is a recent development in Ontario as well as in other provinces. Although 77% of the productive and non-productive forest in northern Ontario can support mixedwoods (BMW sites) and 46% of the land-base is currently in a mixedwood condition (BMW stands) (Towill et al. 2004), few of these stands were managed based on mixedwood objectives. They are mixedwoods more by accident than by design.

Ontario's first silvicultural guide for boreal mixedwoods (OMNR 2003) identified many gaps in the knowledge of mixedwood ecology and management. Given the need to maintain healthy and productive mixedwoods on the landscape, reducing these gaps in a timely manner is critical.

VALUE OF ADAPTIVE MANAGEMENT IN FORESTS

The adaptive approach to forest management originated in the 1970s and 1980s (Holling 1978; Walters 1986). Adaptive management is a process of designed learning, not one of trial and error. It uses appropriate scales for the questions being addressed, as well as operationally based equipment, operators, and scheduling to implement treatments. By keeping scale and implementation in line with normal operational practices, results from adaptive management studies can be quickly incorporated into daily operations.

Passive adaptive management—testing one policy or practice at a time via a "best practices" approach—is common in resource management; it is the form of adaptive management endorsed in Ontario's *Forest Management Planning Manual* (OMNR 2004). In forestry, active adaptive management—testing multiple policies or practices simultaneously—is rare.

STAND LEVEL ADAPTIVE MANAGEMENT (SLAM) MIXEDWOOD PROJECT

Project Origins

Interest in the use of adaptive forest management and discussions on the development and implementation of an operational-scale adaptive management project addressing forestry issues began in the mid-1990s. OMNR conducted a feasibility study (MacDonald et al. 1997) and held a conference on the potential of adaptive management approaches (MacDonald et al. 1999).

In 2000, forest managers expressed interest in the use of alternative management approaches for mixedwood stands. Representatives of government, industry, and non-profit organizations came together to plan and implement the Stand Level Adaptive Management, or SLAM, Mixedwood Project. A workshop was conducted for project partners and external experts to define the most limiting management uncertainties, formulate potential management scenarios (treatment packages), propose indicators for assessing treatment responses, and define partner roles and responsibilities (MacDonald et al. 2003).

Project Objectives

The primary objective of the SLAM project is to assess a series of alternative management approaches to regenerate productive and balanced mixtures of conifers and hardwood trees on BMW sites in northern Ontario while maintaining the ecological integrity of the site.

The study treatment packages were developed by researchers and forest managers to compare

- blended mixtures of tree species with mosaics of alternating hardwood and conifer strips;

- the use of partial cutting with tending to enhance conifer performance in mixedwood stands;

- the relative costs of treatment packages; and

- ecological indicators (vegetation richness, diversity and succession, microclimate, soil and water properties, and invertebrate populations) across treatment packages.

SLAM is also set up to allow examination of a number of ecological parameters that can be used to produce a reliable indicator of ecological sustainability on managed BMW sites.

Project Partners

SLAM's project partners are as follows: Abitibi Consolidated Company of Canada (Iroquois Falls); Domtar Inc. (Timmins); the Forest Engineering Research Institute of Canada, or FERIC; Lake Abitibi Model Forest; the Canadian Forest Service, Great Lakes Forestry Centre (Sault Ste Marie); and the Mixedwood Silviculture Program at the Ontario Forest Research Institute (MacDonald et al. 2003). The roles of partnering organizations are

outlined in Table 1. Of special note is the role of the Lake Abitibi Model Forest, which provides the link to regional stakeholders; this tie to local groups is critical in the development of the project and will be key as transfer activities increase.

Table 1. Stand Level Adaptive Management Mixedwood Project partners and their roles.

Project partner	Main role
Ontario Forest Research Institute	Provide science support (silviculture, succession, soils, water). Lead external funding submissions. Contributes to silvicultural guide revisions.
Canadian Forest Service, Great Lakes Forestry Centre	Provide science support (biodiversity).
Abitibi Consolidated and Domtar[a]	Conduct harvesting and forest renewal. Ensure necessary management plan adjustments are made.
Forest Engineering Research Institute of Canada	Do cost comparisons of treatments.
Lake Abitibi Model Forest	Transfer results to clients and public. Link to regional stakeholders (First Nations, resource users, schools, recreational groups).

[a]Participation of forest companies with different markets and management objectives (desirable species mixes) broadens applicability of results.

Indicators of Treatment Responses

Central to the SLAM project objective is ensuring that the range of forest values is maintained. Monitoring and assessment go beyond tree performance to include a range of ecological parameters as well as an economic comparison. Indicators being monitored and assessed include the following:

Ecological effects

- Vegetation—species richness and evenness indices, and successional patterns.

- Soil/water nutrients—above- and belowground elemental pools, litter inputs and decomposition, and nutrient cycling and leaching.

- Microclimate—temperature, relative humidity, photosynthetically active radiation, wind speed and direction, soil moisture, and temperature.

- Invertebrate diversity—numbers and location of ground and flying beetles and ground spiders. (Note: Invertebrates are being monitored because they are considered an appropriate indicator of ecosystem health and resilience.)

Silvicultural effects

- Regeneration performance—density, stocking, and growth of all regenerating tree species (both natural and planted).

- Residual stand structure—species, diameter distribution, and quality.

Cost comparisons of treatments

- Relative cost—time trials, accepted yield tables, and operation costs.

Project Challenges

As with any large long-term project, many challenges have emerged since the inception of SLAM. At the broadest scale, project barriers were outlined by MacDonald and Rice (2004). Some critical ones are outlined in Table 2 along with challenges to overcoming them.

Progress

Progress on the SLAM project has been steady. To date the following activities have been accomplished:

- All operational treatments (harvest, renewal, tending, etc.) are complete.

- Monitoring of ecological and silvicultural responses to treatments being tested is underway.

- A report on the establishment of the project has been published (MacDonald et al. 2003).

- An economic comparison among treatment packages has been published (Meek and Cormier 2004).

- A journal paper on the adaptive management process has been published (MacDonald and Rice 2004).

- A series of on-site tours for resource managers have occurred and more are planned.

The next milestones will be reached in 2007 when the fifth year of data collection is completed at the Abitibi study site and in 2008 when fifth-year results are collected at the Domtar site.

Ties to the Malawi Principles

During the second meeting of the Conference of Parties to the Convention on Biological Diversity (CBD) in 1995, delegates endorsed an ecosystem approach as the CBD's primary framework for action. At a workshop held in 1998, 12 principles and five operational guidelines were developed to support this approach. These principles and guidelines are known as the Malawi

Table 2. Critical barriers identified for the Stand Level Adaptive Management Mixedwood Project and challenges to overcoming these barriers in the first five years of the project.

Barrier	Challenges
Team building and maintenance	Complexity of team (government, industry, non-government organizations).
	Agreement on common project objectives from partners with widely differing mandates.
	Changes in partners' personnel that resulted in the need for additional education and training on the value of the adaptive management approach.
Field implementation	Complexity (uncertainties) of using a company's normal operational equipment and schedules to implement the project.
	Operational realities (road locations, treatment timing, equipment limitations, etc.) that required partners to be more flexible and adopt consensus-building methods.
Changing priorities	Changes in resource sector and societal priorities since project initiation that required efforts by the partners to maintain the focus and relevance of the project.
Funding commitment[a]	Difficulty of implementing and funding long-term research projects.
	Ongoing search for funding needed to complete monitoring step.

[a] The project has received external funding from the Ontario Living Legacy Trust (2002–04) and the Enhanced Forest Productivity Science Program of the Ontario Forestry Futures Trust (2005–08)

Principles (FAO 2001, CBD 1999) and are discussed in Hendrickson (this publication).

Many of the principles and guidelines outlined in the Malawi Principles have guided the development of the SLAM project. Some became embedded in Ontario's legislation and policies, while others were incorporated in the approach used by the SLAM project. The main ones are as follows:

- Recognizing that mixedwood forests are part of the range of forest types and ages to be maintained across the landscape and that in all management practices biodiversity needs to be conserved (embedded in provincial legislation, such as the *Crown Forest Sustainability Act,* and policy).

- Developing forest management plans at the management unit level where a local citizen's committee is part of the planning process (embedded in the planning process).

- Relying on a broad project team (non-government organizations, or NGOs, government, and industry) to develop sustainable management approaches. One project partner (Lake Abitibi Model Forest) specifically provided a link to local forest stakeholders during project development.

- Monitoring a range of plants, animals, and ecological processes to ensure treatments are silviculturally, ecologically, and economically sustainable.

- Working within an active adaptive management framework of continuous improvement and learning that

  - includes an access <> design <> implement <> monitor <> assess <> adjust cycle; and

  - ties into adjustments in policy and operational practices.

- Working at a spatial scale appropriate for the questions being addressed.

- Recognizing the need for ongoing training and education about approaches and recommended treatments with resource managers and operators.

SUMMARY

The SLAM project was established to reduce uncertainty in the management of boreal mixedwoods in northern Ontario. A diverse project team was assembled including representatives from government, the forest industry, and NGOs, including the Lake Abitibi Model Forest, which has links with a range of local stakeholders.

The project was designed to examine the ecological, economic, and silvicultural effects of treatment packages being tested in an active adaptive management framework. Through provincial legislation, strategic directions, and policy directives, the adaptive management approach, and the intent to examine a range of plants, animals, and ecological processes, SLAM adheres closely to the principles and guidelines for an ecosystem approach to management outlined by the Convention on Biological Diversity (CBD 2000).

REFERENCES

[CBD] Convention on Biological Diversity. 1995. Conference of the Parties. Decision II/8. Preliminary consideration of components of biological diversity particularly under threat and action which could be taken under the Convention. http://www.cbd.int/decisions/cop-02.shtml?m=COP-02&id=7081&lg=0 [Accessed November 2007.]

[CBD] Convention on Biological Diversity. 1999. Subsidiary Body on Scientific, Technical and Technological Advice. Working document. Ecosystem Approach: Further conceptual elaboration. http://www.cbd.int/doc/meetings/sbstta/sbstta-05/official/sbstta-05-11-en.doc [Accessed November 2007.]

[CBD] Convention on Biological Diversity. 2000. Conference of the Parties. Decision V/6. Ecosystem approach. http://www.cbd.int/decisions/cop-05.shtml?m=COP-05&id=7148&lg=0 [Accessed November 2007.]

[CFSA] Crown Forest Sustainability Act. 1994. Bill 171, An Act to revise the Crown Timber Act to provide for the sustainability of Crown forests in Ontario, S.O. Ch. 25. 37 p.

[FAO] Food and Agriculture Organization of the United Nations. 2001. State of the world's forests 2001. FAO, Rome. http://www.fao.org/DOCREP/003/Y0900E/y0900e07.htm [Accessed June 2007.]

Holling, C.S., ed. 1978. Adaptive environmental assessment and management. John Wiley and Sons Ltd., London. 377 p.

MacDonald, G.B. 1995. The case for boreal mixedwood management: An Ontario perspective. For. Chron. 71: 725–734.

MacDonald, G.B.; Arnup, R.; Jones, R.K. 1997. Adaptive forest management in Ontario: A literature review and strategic analysis. Ontario Ministry of Natural Resources, Ontario Forest Research Institute, Sault Ste. Marie, ON. For. Res. Inf. Paper 139. 38 p.

MacDonald, G.B.; Fraser, J.; Gray, P. 1999. Adaptive management forum: Linking management and science to achieve ecological sustainability. Ontario Ministry of Natural Resources, Ontario Forest Research Institute, Sault Ste. Marie, ON. Sci. Dev. Transfer Ser. 001. 58 p.

MacDonald, G.B.; Rice, J.A.. 2004. An active adaptive management case study in Ontario boreal mixedwood stands. For. Chron. 80(3):391–400.

MacDonald, G. B.; Rice, J.A.; McLaughlin, J.; Pearce, J.; Venier, L.; Nystrom, K.; Meek, P. 2003. Developing sustainable mixedwood practices in a stand-level adaptive management (SLAM) framework: Project establishment. Ontario Ministry of Natural Resources, Ontario Forest Research Institute, Sault Ste. Marie, ON. For. Res. Rep. 157. 17 p.

Meek, P.; Cormier, D. 2004. Cost evaluation of four treatments (FERIC contribution to the SLAM project). Forest Engineering Research Institute of Canada (FERIC), Pointe-Claire, QC. Internal Rep. IR-2004-07-30 (Partial cutting program 2120). 14 p.

[OMNR] Ontario Ministry of Natural Resources. 1995. Policy framework for sustainable forests. OMNR, Toronto, ON. 6 p.

[OMNR] Ontario Ministry of Natural Resources. 2003. Silviculture guide to managing spruce, fir, birch, and aspen mixedwoods in Ontario's boreal forest. Version 1.0. OMNR, Toronto, ON. 382 p.

[OMNR] Ontario Ministry of Natural Resources. 2004. Forest management planning manual for Ontario's Crown forests. OMNR, Toronto, ON. 440 p.

[OMNR] Ontario Ministry of Natural Resources. 2005. Our sustainable future: Ministry of Natural Resources strategic directions. OMNR, Toronto, ON. 23 p.

[OMNR] Ontario Ministry of Natural Resources. 2007. Overview of Ontario's forests. OMNR, Toronto, ON. http://ontariosforests.mnr.gov.on.ca/spectrasites/internet/ontarioforests/forestoverview.cfm [Accessed June 2007.]

Towill, W.D.; Wiltshire, R.O.; Desharnais, J.C. 2004. Distribution, extent and importance of boreal mixedwood forests in Ontario. Ontario Ministry of Natural Resources, Toronto, ON. Sci. Technol. Ser. Vol. 9. Boreal Mixedwood Note 4. 14 p.

Walters, C.J. 1986 Adaptive management of renewable resources. Macmillan, New York, NY. 300 p.

New Brunswick's Systems Approach to Natural Resources Management Planning

Steve Gordon Manager, Habitat Program, Fish and Wildlife Branch
New Brunswick Department of Natural Resources, Fredericton, NB

INTRODUCTION

New Brunswick has been applying a systems approach to natural resources management planning on its Crown forest lands for over 20 years. This approach has evolved considerably from the rather timber-centric forest management plans of the early and mid-1980s through to today's Crown land-use review process and forest management plans that deal explicitly with a broad range of timber and non-timber values.

The province's approach continues to evolve (adaptive management), particularly in the area of public input to forest level goals and objectives (GNB 2004). Currently, the strategies used to achieve goals and objectives remain the domain of government and industry foresters, biologists, and policy makers.

NEW BRUNSWICK'S FORESTS

New Brunswick has a landmass of 7.3 million ha of which about 85% is forested, 2% is inland waters, 5% is wetland, 4% is urban or developed, and 4% is agricultural. The majority of New Brunswick falls in the Acadian Forest Region of Canada with some Great Lakes–St. Lawrence and Boreal in the northwest corner of the province. As such, there is a diversity of tree and wildlife species. The province's ecological land classification identifies 7 distinct ecoregions, 35 ecodistricts, and 154 ecosections based on climate, geomorphology, geology, and landform and glacial deposits (Figure 1). There are 13 larger watersheds (24 000–2.9 million ha) and 141 sub-watersheds (214 000–776 000 ha).

Forest Uses

The dominant commercial use of the forest is the provision of wood for the pulp and paper and sawmill industry. Maple sugar production, Christmas tree production, trapping of furbearers, guiding of hunters and fishers, and harvesting of non-traditional forest products (for example, ground hemlock) are other commercial uses. The harvest of forest biomass for energy production is on the horizon. Other commercial uses of forest lands include mineral exploration and mining, gravel pits and quarries, and blueberry production.

Forest lands are also used by citizens and visitors for a variety of recreational pursuits including hunting and fishing, hiking, camping, boating, berry picking, and wildlife viewing. Approximately 1% of the province's land area is located in provincial and national parks.

Forest Ownership

Fifty-one percent of the forest land is provincial Crown land (public land), 29% is private land, 18% is industrial freehold, and 2% is federal land (Figure 2 and NBDNR 2008). The scope of this paper refers to implementation of a systems approach on Crown forest lands only.

LEGISLATION AND POLICIES

It would be extremely difficult to implement a systems approach to natural resources management without supporting policies, principles, and regulations. The key factors that provide the context and set the stage for using a systems approach on New Brunswick Crown land are discussed below.

The 3.2 million ha of Crown forest land are administered by the New Brunswick Department of Natural Resources (NBDNR) under the *Crown Lands and Forests Act* (GNB 1982). In addition to the administration of Crown lands and forests, NBDNR is responsible for the regulation and management of fish and wildlife resources, mineral exploration and mining, and among other responsibilities is the lead agency for biodiversity conservation. The broad mandate of the NBDNR enhances the opportunity for cross-sectoral communications, planning, and the integrated management of the forest.

The *Crown Lands and Forests Act* (section 3(1)) gives the minister responsibility for the development, protection, and integrated management of the resources of Crown lands, including

a) access to and travel on Crown lands,

b) harvesting and renewal of timber resources on Crown lands,

c) habitat for the maintenance of fish and wildlife populations,

d) forest recreation on Crown lands,

e) rehabilitation of Crown lands, and

f) other matters that may be assigned under this act or the regulations.

NBDNR sets management goals, objectives, and standards for Crown land and evaluates Crown Timber Licensee (Licensee) performance (NBDNR 2005a).

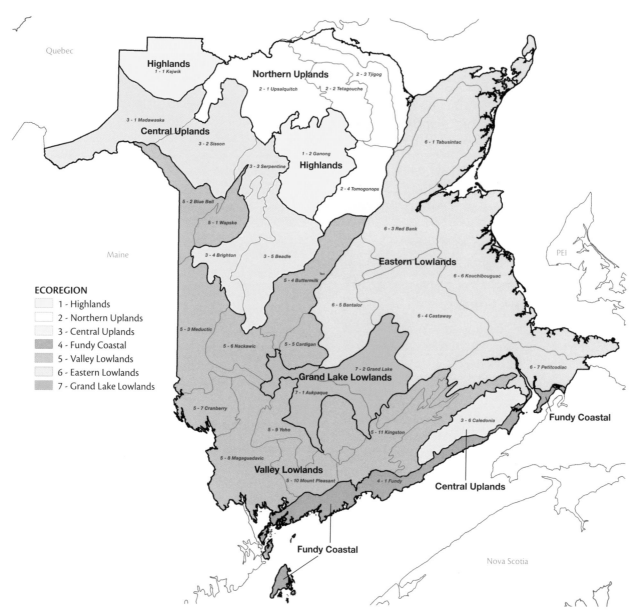

Figure 1. Ecoregion and ecodistrict boundaries of New Brunswick.

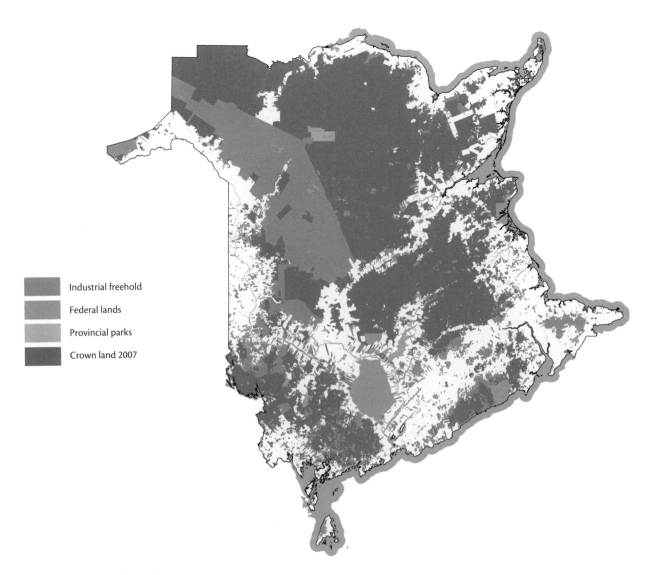

Figure 2. Landownership in New Brunswick.

The act divides the Crown forest into 10 Crown Timber Licenses (Licenses) that are managed by Licensees under the terms and conditions of 25-year Forest Management Agreements. A management plan must be developed every five years (for each License). The plan outlines the objectives for which Crown land resources will be used by the Licensee and the manner in which the Licensee will manage the lands over the 25-year period. Licensees periodically report on their forest management activities and the renewal of Forest Management Agreements is based on an evaluation of five-year plans against NBDNR objectives and standards (NBDNR 2005a).

FOREST MANAGEMENT PLANS

Today's forest management plans deal explicitly with multiple values related to the concept of ecosystem-based management: wood supply, forest diversity, wildlife habitat, water quality and aquatic habitat, and forest aesthetics.

The values, goals, objectives, standards, and responsibilities for forest management plans are published every five years; the most recent was in 2005 for the 2007 forest management plans: The New Brunswick Public Forest—Our shared future (NBDNR 2005a) and Objectives and Standards for the New Brunswick Crown Forest for the 2007–2012 Period (NBDNR 2005b). The values and goals for which there are explicit strategies and objectives incorporated into forest management planning on Crown land include

- wood supply

- forest diversity

- wildlife habitat

- water quality and aquatic habitat and

- aesthetics and recreation.

Though forest management plans are prepared and implemented by License, objectives for forest diversity and wildlife habitat are defined at the scale of ecodistrict and ecoregion. The License is the planning unit for wood supply.

Aquatic habitat and water quality values are dealt with through standard watercourse buffer rules (NBDNR 2004). Watersheds that supply municipal drinking water are designated under law and have a more restrictive set of land-use and watercourse protection standards (NBENV 2007).

Day-to-day operational policies and standards ranging from road building and natural regeneration standards to deer-wintering area management are described in the Forest Management Manual for New Brunswick Crown Land (NBDNR 2004). NBDNR develops these standards cooperatively with Licensees.

Balancing Uses of Crown Lands

Essential to the systems approach is integrating the demands and effects on the forest of other forest uses. These non-forestry uses contribute to the multiple-use aspects of forest management and can pose significant challenges to sustaining forest values. The allocation of Crown forest lands for non-forestry purposes in New Brunswick, such as parks, wind energy, mining, and campsite leases, occurs outside the forest management planning process, as part of a land-use review process. The process provides the opportunity for responsible NBDNR programs to identify impacts to other values and uses (that is, species at risk, wildlife habitat, wood supply, recreation, biodiversity). Land-use decisions, including the acquisition and disposal of Crown lands, are made in the context of NBDNR's mandate, goals, and policies, and those of the provincial government as a whole.

Those uses of the forest of most concern to the concept of ecosystem-based management are ones that change the forest (for example, mine sites). Less than 0.5% of Crown land (approximately 11 000 ha) is currently allocated to mine sites, pits, and quarries (R. Shaw and M.

O'Donnell, NBDNR, Fredericton, NB, personal communication). Other allocated lands include 4500 km of hiking, snowmobiling, and ATV trails and 15 000 ha of campsite, maple sugary, and blueberry leases, the total area representing approximately 0.5% of Crown land (NBDNR 2008).

In New Brunswick, these other forest land uses affect less than 1% of Crown land and though some have a detrimental effect on wood supply, forest diversity, wildlife habitat, or aesthetics at the site level, they do not pose a significant challenge to sustaining forest values on Crown land.

The goals and objectives and the strategies to deliver them are described briefly. These are implemented through the forest management plans for each License. The plans forecast wood supply, forest diversity, and wildlife habitat values for 80 years; spatially identify timber harvest blocks for 25 years; identify two large patch size wildlife habitats for 35 years; and identify deer-wintering areas, old-forest vegetation communities, watercourse and wetland buffer zones, and protected natural areas for 80 years. Figure 3 shows the spatial layout of forest identified to meet forest diversity and wildlife habitat objectives in the 2007 forest management plans for Crown land.

Wood Supply

The goal for the 2007 forest management plans is to maintain the softwood annual allowable cut (AAC) at 2002 levels. There is no stated goal related to hardwood.

The provincial spruce, fir, and jack pine AAC will be maintained at the levels established in 2002. Work is being undertaken to develop a comprehensive set of softwood and hardwood wood supply objectives for the 2012 forest management plans.

The strategy has been to maximize the sustainable non-declining flow of softwood fiber from each License while achieving all other non-timber objectives and thresholds. The sustainable supply of hardwood is maximized after the softwood AAC is established. Both are supported by a program of planting, pre-commercial thinning, and stand tending.

Even-aged silviculture systems dominate conifer forest management and clearcutting is the dominant harvest

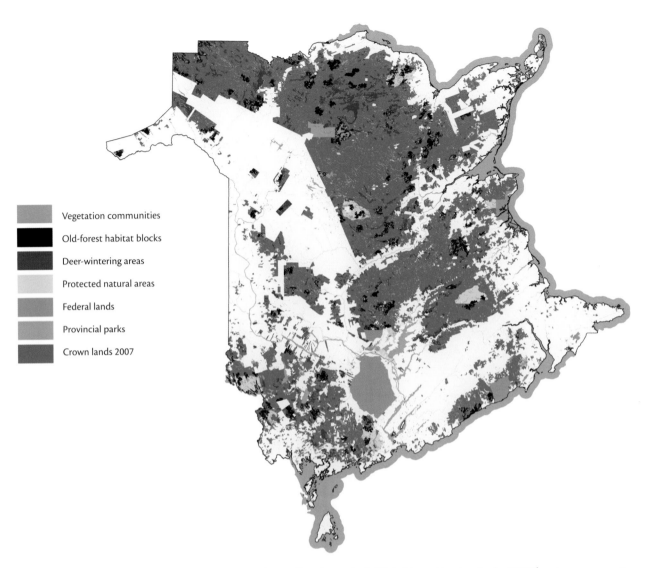

Figure 3. Spatial layout of forest identified to meet forest diversity and wildlife habitat objectives in the 2007 forest management plans for New Brunswick Crown land.

Legend:
- Vegetation communities
- Old-forest habitat blocks
- Deer-wintering areas
- Protected natural areas
- Federal lands
- Provincial parks
- Crown lands 2007

prescription. The deciduous forest is managed using a more even mix of uneven-aged and even-aged silviculture systems and partial harvesting is a more common prescription.

Forest Diversity

The goal is to maintain the natural diversity and ecological characteristics of the Acadian forest. There are two objectives: 1) New Brunswick has identified approximately 150 000 ha of Crown forest land as fine-filter and coarse-filter protected natural areas; 2) minimum thresholds (hectares) exist for the abundance of 12 broad forest types to be maintained in an old-forest condition by License and ecoregion. The thresholds are equal to 12% of the total area (all development stages) in each forest type.

The strategy for maintaining forest diversity uses two tactics: 1) protected areas directed at unique sites (stand level) and representative areas (ecoregion representation), and 2) old-forest representation by broad forest type where compatible timber harvesting is permitted. Implementing the objective by ecoregion helps to ensure some level of forest type variability across the landscape.

Wildlife Habitat

The goal is to provide the habitat necessary to support populations of native wildlife at desired levels across a natural range of a species on Crown lands. There are two objectives. The first is to determine minimum thresholds (hectares) are defined for six old-forest wildlife habitats by License and ecoregion to focus on the needs of 45 bird and mammal species. The other objective is to establish and manage 900 deer-wintering areas totaling 260 000 ha of forest to provide winter habitat to support enough white-tailed deer for hunting.

The strategy has been to focus on wildlife requiring old forest because its abundance is being reduced significantly through timber harvesting for wood products (Figure 4 and NBDNR 1995). Habitats are defined in terms of stand structure, patch size, and interpatch distances (NBDNR 2005c).

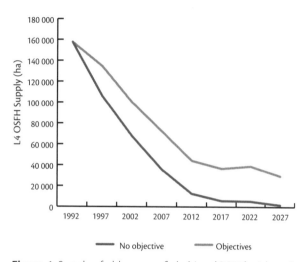

Figure 4. Supply of old spruce–fir habitat (OSFH) with and without the implementation of habitat objectives from the 1992 forest management plans for License 4; OSFH patch size is ≥ 375 ha and the threshold on License 4 is 26 500 ha.

Habitat thresholds are at levels considered sufficient to maintain healthy (viable) populations of associated wildlife across the ecodistricts and ecoregions of Crown land in which they traditionally occur. Five hundred breeding pairs have been used to define the minimum viable population size for individual species.

Forest management plans ensure thresholds are met or exceeded for the 80-year planning time frame. The two old-forest wildlife habitats with large patch size requirements (375 ha) are mapped for the first 35 years of the management plan. Timber harvesting is permitted in all habitats following specific standards.

Water Quality and Aquatic Habitat

The goal is to protect water quality and maintain aquatic habitat for associated fish and wildlife species. There are no quantified objectives or thresholds related to this goal.

Buffer zones ranging from 30 to 60 m wide are maintained adjacent to watercourses and wetlands. Timber harvesting (partial harvests) is permitted in buffer zones following specific standards.

Aesthetics

The goal is to maintain the aesthetic appeal of the forest for users of high-use recreational waters and highways traversing Crown lands. There are no quantified objectives or thresholds related to this goal.

Buffer zones ranging from 30 to 90 m wide are maintained adjacent to high-use recreational waters and 30-m buffers are maintained adjacent to highways crossing Crown lands. Timber harvesting (partial harvests) is permitted following specific standards.

Gaps and Challenges

Institutions

Institutionally, it would be beneficial to formalize the framework for land-use planning within NBDNR and include outside agencies with overlapping mandates. For example, as the federal authority for the *Migratory Birds Convention Act*, the Canadian Wildlife Service has an overlapping mandate to conserve healthy populations of migratory birds. A formal framework would improve communication between sectors and set expectations for inclusion and contributions. It would also facilitate proactive rather than reactive planning regarding non-forestry uses of Crown land, such as parks or mining leases.

Once government agencies step beyond the comfort of Crown land, they run into the challenges of influencing private land use and management. Formalized land-use planning structures that incorporate ecological-based planning units and identify how various land users interface would be beneficial. Because approximately 50% of the province is privately owned, a systems approach that includes private lands is desirable to achieve biodiversity and sustainable use goals.

Science and Monitoring

Good applied science has never been needed more than in the science-based decision-making world we work in today. Though New Brunswick is still 85%

forested, all but 4% of the forest is available to be harvested in some manner. Therefore, it is important to have research (ideally local) that answers questions related to the forest structures (stand and forest level) needed to maintain forest diversity and other values. This is true for other biomes as well.

Once a management program is in place, the human and monetary resources that conceptualized it and got it successfully underway are often caught up in supporting its day-to-day implementation. The rigorous monitoring and assessment needed to inform adaptive management are often left lacking, whereas they should be part of the plan from the beginning.

KEY LESSONS

Clear Mandate Essential

A clearly stated mandate and vision provides the necessary top-down direction for those at the program level to do their job. In New Brunswick, we have relied on the statement in the *Crown Lands and Forests Act* pertaining to habitat for the maintenance of fish and wildlife populations to provide the legal backbone for putting in place forest diversity and wildlife habitat objectives and strategies. Policy makers of the late 1970s and 1980s showed great insight by including this statement in the act. Without it, managing for forest diversity and wildlife habitat would be a "good thing" but not a legally based requirement.

Once the mandate is defined, all that is needed is the supporting programs with clear areas of responsibility working together. At NBDNR, there is a strong working relationship between the programs in Fish and Wildlife and Forest Management branches and the Licensees.

Quantified Objectives and Thresholds Crucial

Critical to the approach used in New Brunswick is the establishment of quantified thresholds and forest structure definitions related to forest diversity and habitat values. They allow forest managers to know what forest stands provide what and how much is needed. A quantitative analysis also provides the opportunity for researchers to test the validity of relationships and assumptions.

To understand the danger of not quantifying your needs, you only have to look to the wood supply side of the equation. Though it would seem all is well when you have a goal to maximize wood supply, it does not guarantee wood supply will not decrease from one management plan to the next (Figure 5). This has spurred the wood industry and government to develop wood supply thresholds for the 2012 Crown forest management plans.

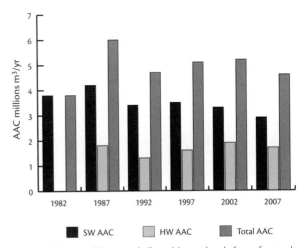

Figure 5. Sustainable annual allowable cut levels for softwood (SW AAC) and hardwood (HW AAC) from New Brunswick Crown forest based on management plans from 1982 to 2007. (Note 2007 AAC values do not include mitigation and accelerated harvest volumes.)

The inclusion of spatial objectives for 170 000 ha of older conifer forest for wildlife along with deer-wintering areas and watercourse buffer zones occurred in 1992. These were largely responsible for the decrease in softwood AAC between 1987 and 1992.

Objectives for five additional old-forest wildlife habitats, eight old-forest vegetation communities, protected natural areas, and wetland buffers followed in later plans. These negatively affected wood supply as well, approximately 5% between 1997 and 2007. Changes to forest growth and yield relationships and harvest treatment eligibilities from one management plan to the next also contribute to changes in sustainable AAC.

Never Too Soon to Act

A lesson learned is the importance of dealing with concerns when they first materialize. Although it is desirable to have science identify an issue and then work toward its resolution, this is rarely the case. Problems must usually be dealt with long before definitive science is available. Waiting only reduces options and ultimately increases the costs of solutions.

REFERENCES

[GNB] Government of New Brunswick. 1982. *Crown Lands and Forests Act*. Fredericton, NB. 66 p. http://www.gnb.ca/acts/acts/c-38-1.htm [Accessed January 2008.]

[GNB] Government of New Brunswick. 2004. Select Committee on Wood Supply—Final report on wood supply. Fredericton, NB. 46 p. http://www.gnb.ca/legis/business/committees/reports/Wood/legwoodfinal-e.pdf [Accessed January 2008.]

[NBDNR] New Brunswick Department of Natural Resources. 1995. Management of forest habitat in New Brunswick. Fredericton, NB. 40 p.

[NBDNR] New Brunswick Department of Natural Resources. 2004. Forest Management Manual for New Brunswick Crown Land. Fredericton, NB. 137 p. http://www.gnb.ca/0078/publications/ForestManagementManual-e.pdf#pagemode=bookmarks [Accessed January 2008.]

[NBDNR] New Brunswick Department of Natural Resources. 2005a. The New Brunswick Public Forest—Our shared future. Fredericton, NB. 8 p. http://142.139.24.21/e-repository/monographs/30000000043979/30000000043979.pdf [Accessed January 2008.]

[NBDNR] New Brunswick Department of Natural Resources. 2005b. Objectives and Standards for the New Brunswick Crown Forest for the 2007–2012 Period. Fredericton, NB. 40 p.

[NBDNR] New Brunswick Department of Natural Resources. 2005c. Habitat Definitions for Old-Forest Vertebrates in New Brunswick. Fredericton, NB. 14 p. http://www.gnb.ca/0078/publications/habitat-e.pdf [Accessed January 2008.]

[NBDNR] New Brunswick Department of Natural Resources. 2008. Forest Report 2007. Fredericton, NB. 7 p. http://www.gnb.ca/0079/ForestReport-e.asp [Accessed January 2008.]

[NBENV] New Brunswick Environment. 2007. A guide to New Brunswick's watershed protected area designation order. Fredericton, NB. 15 p. http://www.gnb.ca/0009/0371/0004/watershed-e.pdf [Accessed January 2008.]

Implementing Ecosystem-based Integrated Resource Management in Nova Scotia

Bruce Stewart Forest Ecologist
Nova Scotia Department of Natural Resources, Truro, NS

Peter Neily Forest Ecologist
Nova Scotia Department of Natural Resources, Truro, NS

INTRODUCTION

Development of a systematic approach to ecosystem-based integrated resource management has been ongoing in Nova Scotia since the early 1990s, supported by the National Forest Strategy (CCFM 1992) and the Canadian Biodiversity Strategy (Environment Canada 1995). The planning system has evolved over this period with the development of ecological planning tools, forest modeling capability, policy guidance, and regulations. Many of the components are well established, some are in use at draft stages, while others are still concepts requiring further development.

Nova Scotia has a land area of 5.3 million ha of which 28% is provincially owned (NSDNR 1999a). The Department of Natural Resources (DNR) has broad responsibilities for a wide range of Crown resources, including timber and forests, wildlife, wildlife reserves, endangered species, fire and pest protection, provincial parks, beaches, and mineral resources. The province is 80% forested, and forestry activities dominate most of the land base (NSDNR 1999a). As a result, many planning tools and systems have a strong forestry focus. Integrated resource management planning promotes synergy between the management of multiple values and encourages the modification of forestry practices for use as efficient tools to meet other management objectives (for example, conservation, habitat). This has increased management options, reduced conflict, and lessened the mitigation required to sustain sensitive values.

The following describes Nova Scotia's progress in implementing ecosystem-based management. A hierarchical ecological planning framework is provided by Nova Scotia's ecological land classification (Neily et. al. 2003). The province's forest ecosystem classification guidebooks provide the stand level extension for management prescriptions (Keys et. al. 2003). A forest modeling system capable of tracking multiple values at various spatial and temporal scales was developed to support planning, and the assessment of forest management strategies. The overall planning system relies on a hierarchical integrated resource management approach that consists of strategic, tactical, and operational levels (NSDNR 2003). Resource planning is governed by a range of acts, regulations, and policies.

The Department of Natural Resources recently began developing new strategies for forests, minerals, parks, and biodiversity (NSDNR 2007b) with extensive public consultation led by a Voluntary Planning Project Committee (NSDNR 2007a). The process will culminate in 2010 with new strategies that will affect the planning system currently conceived and described in this paper.

ECOSYSTEM CLASSIFICATION FRAMEWORK

The ecological framework consists of several classifications and interpretations:

- The **ecological land classification (ELC) for Nova Scotia** was designed to support a broad range of ecosystem management planning issues and scales (Table 1) (Neily et al. 2003). It has five nested hierarchical levels each defined by a set of enduring features that increase in number and precision from the continental scale to the local scale.

- **Natural disturbance regime** and **potential climax forest interpretations** were developed to provide knowledge of pre-European conditions and processes (Neily et al. 2007). These interpretations are attached to the ecosection level of the ELC, making them easily mapped, readily adaptable to new information, and explicitly linked to enduring ecological features. They will inform planning at both landscape and stand scales respecting forest composition, age structure, patch size, successional development, and harvesting systems.

- A **forest ecosystem classification (FEC)** provides site level descriptions of ecotypes, vegetation types, and soil types (Keys et. al. 2003). Three interim guidebooks have been produced that provide fairly complete coverage of the province. The full system, with guidebooks for each ecoregion, is scheduled for completion in 2010. The FEC system is the stand level extension of the ELC and will be incorporated into operational prescriptions affecting vegetation development and soil conservation.

Table 1. Management applications for the ecological land classification for Nova Scotia.

EcoUnit	Management application
Ecozone	The province is entirely contained within the Acadian forest ecozone, a continental unit used for developing and coordinating strategic policies at regional, national, and international levels.
Ecoregion	Nine provincial climatic regions support distinctive vegetation communities and physiographic patterns. Ecoregions will be used to roll up landscape plans produced for ecodistricts into "master" landscapes to address coarse-scale issues related to habitat conditions, timber flow, etc.
Ecodistrict	Thirty-nine ecodistricts are characterized by distinctive patterns of vegetation, landform, and ecological processes. These provide the landscape units used for tactical planning.
Ecosection	Consistent physical conditions support repeating vegetation communities and successional responses. The pattern of repetition across ecodistricts imparts character and shapes landscape processes. Ecosections provide the fundamental unit for describing landscape structure and analyzing functions. This level of classification includes natural disturbance regime and potential climax forest interpretations, as well as non-forest communities.
Ecosite	Ecosites have not yet been mapped and are expected to be similar to the ecotypes described in the forest ecosystem classification guidebooks. These units will support operational planning and fine-scale conservation.

- A hierarchical **vegetation classification** is evolving to integrate existing forest and non-forest classifications and inventories. It will include vegetation types, successional stage and pathways interpretations, natural disturbance processes, growth projections, and ecosystem associations.

INTEGRATED RESOURCE MANAGEMENT PLANNING SYSTEM

An integrated resource management (IRM) process was developed to coordinate planning among resource sectors to optimize multiple benefits and minimize conflicts (NSDNR 2003). This consists of a strategic, tactical, and operational planning system led by Department of Natural Resources IRM teams composed of professional and technical experts from minerals, forests, recreation, wildlife, and parks.

Strategic

Public and stakeholder consultations were completed in 2002 to identify issues and inventory values on Crown land. Over 1500 submissions were received and results were compiled to produce two planning products designed to inform tactical and operational planning:

1. Spatial classification of all Crown land to identify primary values and areas with overlapping and potentially conflicting values (NSDNR 2003)

   C1 General Resource Use (507 000 ha, source IRM data 2007).

   C2 Multiple and Adaptive Resource Use consisting of specific resource value categories (671 000 ha)

   C3 Protected and Limited Use (303 000 ha). Most is administered by the Department of Environment and Labour under the Wilderness Areas Program

2. A statement of 24 provincial objectives, with associated strategies and indicators, representing management priorities for seven sectors: water, land, multiresource, conservation and recreation, minerals and energy, wildlife, and forestry.

Tactical

Development of long-range management frameworks involves a two-step process that begins with an ecological landscape analysis (Stewart and Neily 2006) and is followed by landscape design. Planning is assisted by the Crown Lands Forest Model decision-support system and the ecological emphasis classification zoning system.

Ecological landscape analysis

Multidisciplinary teams from the Department of Natural Resources conduct an ecological landscape analysis for the entire land base in each of the province's 39 forested ecodistricts (Stewart and Neily 2006). These analyses provide a foundation for ecosystem-based planning on Crown land and will be made publicly available as a resource for private land planners seeking a common ecological framework. The analysis closely follows the procedures outlined by Diaz and Apostol (1992) with modifications to fit the Nova Scotia condition as follows:

- **The landscape as an ecological system:** landscape structure in terms of matrix, patch, and corridor ecosystems is defined, and the relationship of landscape flows and functions to the ecological structure is explored.

- **Connectivity and fragmentation:** the nature of connectivity within the landscape is characterized.

- **Special features:** rare, uncommon, and threatened species; sites, habitats, and other sublandscape scale features are identified.

- **Ecological representation:** the distribution of ecological units (ELC) and communities within reserve systems is quantified.

- **Road ecology:** a road index tool is used to quantify and map the relative ecological influence of the transportation network, and identify potential intersections with ecological systems.

- **Landscape composition:** the landbase classification from the forest model is used to summarize the current distribution of vegetation communities, age classes, and successional stages.

- **Ecological emphasis classification:** the current distribution of ecological emphasis classes is mapped using geographic information system (GIS) inventory and previous treatment records. An ecological emphasis index is summarized at various ecological levels to quantify relative land-use intensity.

Landscape design

Landscape design provides a best fit of preferred ecosystem management direction that will need to integrate ecology, forest management, mineral, park, and biodiversity objectives to achieve a balance of social, economic, and environmental values within ecodistricts and ecoregions. Opportunities and constraints are highlighted and options for action defined. Landscape design products include spatial representation of current and future land uses along with management directives and activity schedules. A broad range of stakeholder interests are intimately involved in this process. Currently, the landscape design procedures are being developed while the landscape analysis proceeds.

Crown lands forest model

The Crown Lands Forest Model provides decision support for landscape-level ecosystem-based planning, and facilitates the design of the forest management component of IRM (that is, preservation/harvest systems/silviculture investment). The model's structure is based on the representation of values and objectives in the form of quantitative indicators. These indicators are an expression of forest condition in spatial and temporal context. The modeling environment allows teams to evaluate management scenarios in the process of selecting or recommending preferred management direction.

Development of the Crown Lands Forest Model is driven by the scope of IRM values. The process of quantifying IRM values within the modeling framework has resulted in:

- A provincial Strategic Forest Modeling Values document that details a suite of standard values, objectives, and indicators that are reflective of current resource management strategies and policies (O'Keefe 2007). The indicators are quantifiable, predictable, and measurable representations of forest conditions relevant for modeling multiple values and objectives.

- A provincial landbase classification process that merges and standardizes the representation of all spatial and attribute databases relevant to IRM values. This provides a consistent representation of existing information for decision makers as well as the initialization necessary for forest projections.

- A forest modeling environment developed on the Remsoft Spatial Planning Systems technology. This modeling environment is the analytical framework that allows the forecasting of forest modeling indicators. A key design functionality is the ability to investigate long-term trends among multiple and often competing forest values and alternative management strategies in developing forest management direction.

Ecological emphasis classification and index

The ecological emphasis classification (EEC) is a planning tool for assessing and assigning classes of land-use intensity (Stewart and Neily 2006). It was incorporated into the growth functions of the Crown Lands Forest Model for evaluating zoning scenarios. An associated ecological emphasis index provides a numerical indicator and monitoring function. Four ecological emphasis classes are defined based on the degree to which management practices emphasize the conservation of natural conditions (Table 2). Two of the classes, intensive and extensive, involve active forest management. The Code of Forest Practice (NSDNR 2004) will provide ecosystem-specific interpretations (based on the FEC) that will specify operational criteria for each ecological emphasis class. Full implementation of the code will not occur until the department's strategy development process is completed in 2010.

Table 2. Ecological emphasis classification (EEC) and index definition (Stewart and Neily 2006).

EEC	Description	Index weight
Reserve	Preservation of natural conditions using laws and policies to restrict management (for example, wilderness, parks, conservation easement, Old Forest Policy).	1
Extensive management	Management of multiple values using ecosystem-based techniques that sustain or restore natural conditions and processes.	0.75
Intensive management	Management to optimize resource production and site productivity on sites maintained in a native state (for example, forested).	0.25
Converted industrial	Conversion to an unnatural state, or significant degradation of site productivity (for example, agriculture, urban, roads, Christmas trees, seed orchards).	0

During the ecological landscape analysis, the condition of all lands is assessed to determine their existing ecological emphasis class reflective of previous use. An ecological emphasis index is then summarized to provide an overall indicator of current land-use intensity.

During the landscape design phase, the EEC is assigned to land units as a zoning tool to guide future activities. Management prescriptions are then governed by the EEC specific requirements contained within the Code of Forest Practice. This has broad application for directing management to meet landscape and local scale objectives (for example, timber, restoration, connectivity).

Operational

Landscape designs are to be implemented through short-range plans and prescriptions that represent the tactical level activity schedules of the different resource sectors. Plans from the forestry sector integrate multiple values, are ecosystem based at the ecosection and ecosite levels, and are subject to review and approval by IRM teams. They may be developed by tenure or rights holders assigned management responsibility for Crown land or resources. Forestry plans will need to conform to Code of Forest Practice guidelines and include site descriptions, treatment prescriptions, and spatial layouts. These procedures are currently being developed and are awaiting completion of the Code of Forest Practice. The following represents the most recent draft:

- Pre-treatment assessment using the FEC.

- Handbooks to determine ecotype, vegetation type, and soil type.

- Harvesting and silviculture prescriptions incorporating FEC specific interpretations and response projections.

- Harvesting and silviculture prescriptions compliant with the EEC zoning requirements and Code of Forest Practice guidelines.

- Harvesting and silviculture prescriptions consistent with the landscape design objectives for forest composition, as reflected in the activity schedules of the Crown Lands Forest Model.

REGULATORY AND POLICY FRAMEWORK

Nova Scotia's resource planning system is supported and guided by a wide array of acts, regulations, and policies. Some of the more recent developments follow.

The *Crown Lands Act*, amended in 1989, provides for the use of Crown lands by governing forest management and harvesting, leasing and licensing, integration of wildlife and recreation in forest management planning, and administration and management of all Crown lands (Nova Scotia 1989).

The *Forests Act* was amended in 1998 to allow for new regulations supporting the 1997 forest strategy (NSDNR 1997, 2007c). A significant component of the strategy was the provision of a Code of Forest Practice, which specifies requirements for management of Crown lands. The code consists of three parts:

- Code Principles provide guidance for strategic planning in the areas of forest ecosystems, forest products, wildlife habitat, and integrated forest use. These principles were released in 2004 (NSDNR 2004).

- Code Guidelines specify management requirements for ecosystems, forest products, wildlife, and integrated use. The code guidebooks are scheduled to be released in draft for public comment in 2008 through the voluntary planning strategy consultation process.

- Technical References developed through research and practice provide tools and options for management applicable to Nova Scotia forest conditions. This includes a broad suite of existing and developing management and decision-support tools.

The *Environmental Goals and Sustainable Prosperity Act*, 2007, recently established several specific initiatives and objectives affecting management of provincial lands (Nova Scotia 2007). The IRM process will need to reflect these objectives:

- commit to legally protect 12% of the provincial land mass by 2015,

- develop a policy preventing loss of wetlands by 2009,

- adopt a natural resources strategy for forests, mines, parks, and biodiversity by 2010.

The Interim Old Forest Policy, 1999, established an objective to identify and protect the best remaining old forests and old-forest restoration opportunities on a minimum 8% of Crown land in each of the 39 ecodistricts (NSDNR 1999b). Most of this objective has now been met.

The Environmental Certification Programs, particularly the Forest Stewardship Council, the Canadian Standards Association, and the Sustainable Forestry Initiative, have a growing influence on forest management direction on private land, which makes up over 70% of the provincial land base. Many of the tools and planning processes developed for Crown IRM support these certification programs which are encouraging better landscape level coordination across tenures. Large areas of Nova Scotia Crown land have already been certified under one or more of these programs.

SUMMARY

Integrated resource management was introduced in the early 1990s as a three-tiered strategic, tactical, and operational planning system. Development of this ecosystem-based approach is evolving as the required planning tools and processes are introduced. This has presented challenges to maintain momentum, integrate planning tools, and provide training and communication in the face of change. Yet the policy has encouraged overall integration of values, better communication among resource sectors, and improved decision-making within the NSDNR.

Currently, the ecological framework and many of the ecosystem planning tools are completed or sufficiently advanced to be in use. The strategic planning phase was completed in February 2002 following public consultation. This produced a spatial land-use classification and a statement of 24 objectives, strategies, and indicators to guide integrated planning across seven sectors. IRM teams currently rely on these products to assess proposals and plan operations while the other planning levels are developed. The tactical level phase was divided into two stages of landscape level planning. An ecological landscape analysis of the province's 39 ecodistricts began in 2007. This will be followed by a landscape design and decision stage for which procedures are currently being finalized. Revision of the operational planning system will follow. Monitoring procedures for tracking progress will use elements from the planning system, including the strategic plan indicators, indexes from the tactical plan, quantifiable values from the forest model, and state of the forest reporting.

Continued progress in implementing the full system relies on policy direction from the Code of Forest Practice which will undergo public consultation as part of the resource strategy initiative. Effective resource management policies in Nova Scotia require sharing and coordination among the three major ownerships, Crown, large private, and small private, each of which make up significant portions of the province. Multistakeholder involvement and coordinated research and planning are other critical components. Progress is occurring with the sharing of ecological tools and classifications and the growing influence of environmental certification programs. This was further enhanced by the emergence of partnership organizations such as the Nova Forest Alliance (Canadian Model Forest Network and Forest Communities Program) in central Nova Scotia; Mersey Tobeatic Research Institute and associated Southwest Nova Biosphere Reserve Association in western Nova Scotia; and the Collaborative Environmental Planning Protection Initiative in eastern Nova Scotia. Many other community partnerships have also developed and will play an important role in the future development of integrated resource management.

REFERENCES

[CCFM] Canadian Council of Forest Ministers. 1992. Sustainable forests: A Canadian commitment. National forest strategy 1992. For. Can., Ottawa, ON. 51 p.

Diaz, N.; Apostol, D. 1992. Forest landscape analysis and design: A process for developing and implementing land management objectives for landscape patterns. USDA Forest Service, Pacific Northwest Region. PNW-R6-ECO-TP-043-92. Portland, OR. Part A, 60 p.; Part B, 58 p. http://www.fs.fed.us/pnw/pubs/flad/ [Accessed January 2008.]

Environment Canada. 1995. Canadian biodiversity strategy: Canada's response to the Convention on Biological Diversity 1995. Minister of Supply and Services Canada. Biodiversity Convention Office, Environment Canada. Hull, QC. 80 p.

Keys, K.; Neily, P.D.; Quigley, E.; Stewart, B. 2003. Forest ecosystem classification of Nova Scotia's model forest. Nova Forest Alliance, Stewiacke, Nova Scotia.

Neily, P.D.; Quigley, E.; Benjamin, L.; Stewart, B.J.; Duke, T. 2003. Ecological land classification for Nova Scotia: Volume 1—Mapping Nova Scotia's terrestrial ecosystems. NSDNR Report DNR 2003-2. Stewiacke, Nova Scotia. 83 p. www.gov.ns.ca/natr/FORESTRY/ecosystem/pdf/ELCrevised2.pdf

Neily, P.D; Quigley, E.J.; Stewart, B.J.; Keys, K.S. 2007. Forest disturbance ecology in Nova Scotia. Draft report 7 February 2007. Renewable Resources Branch, Forestry Division, Ecosystem Management Group. Stewiacke, Nova Scotia. Unpublished report.

Nova Scotia. 1989. Crown Lands Act: Chapter 114 of the revised statutes, 1989. Office of the Legislative Counsel, Nova Scotia House of Assembly. http://www.gov.ns.ca/legislature/legc/statutes/crownlan.htm [Accessed January 2008.]

Nova Scotia. 2007. Environmental Goals and Sustainable Prosperity Act: Chapter 7 of the acts of 2007. Office of the Legislative Counsel, Nova Scotia House of Assembly. www.gov.ns.ca/legislature/legc/bills/60th_1st/3rd_read/b146.htm [Accessed January 2008.]

[NSDNR] Nova Scotia Department of Natural Resources. 1997. Towards sustainable forestry: A position paper. Working paper, 1997–2001. 41 p. http://www.gov.ns.ca/NATR/publications/forpubs.htm#nsfp [Accessed January 2008.]

[NSDNR] Nova Scotia Department of Natural Resources.1999a. Forest resources inventory report: Sept 1999. NSDNR Renewable Resources/Forestry Division. Report FOR1991-1. Halifax, NS. 29 p. + tables.

[NSDNR] Nova Scotia Department of Natural Resources. 1999b. Nova Scotia's old growth forests: interim old forest policy. www.gov.ns.ca/natr/forestry/planresch/oldgrowth/policy.htm [Accessed January 2008.]

[NSDNR] Nova Scotia Department of Natural Resources. 2003. Guidelines for the development of long range management frameworks. DNR Manual 2003-1. Halifax, NS. 43 p.

[NSDNR] Nova Scotia Department of Natural Resources. 2004. Nova Scotia's Code of Forest Practice: A framework for the implementation of sustainable forest management. Report For2004-8. www.gov.ns.ca/natr/forestry/strategy/code/NScodeofprac.pdf [Accessed January 2008.]

[NSDNR] Nova Scotia Department of Natural Resources. 2007a. Natural resources strategy: Public engagement project overview. Voluntary Planning, A Citizens' Policy Forum. http://vp.gov.ns.ca/projects/resources [Accessed February 2008.]

[NSDNR] Nova Scotia Department of Natural Resources. 2007b. Natural resources strategy development begins. http://www.gov.ns.ca/news/details.asp?id=20070501004 [Accessed January 2008.]

[NSDNR] Nova Scotia Department of Natural Resources. 2007c. Nova Scotia's forest strategy. http://www.gov.ns.ca/natr/forestry/strategy/default.htm [Accessed January 2008.]

O'Keefe, R. 2007. Statement of strategic forest modeling values. Integrated Resource Management, Forest Modeling Committee. NSDNR Forestry Division. Truro, NS. Unpublished draft.

Stewart, B.J.; Neily, P.D. 2006. A procedural guide for ecological landscape analysis: an ecosystem-based approach to landscape level planning in Nova Scotia. NSDNR. Truro, NS. Unpublished report.

A National Ecosystem Approach and Integrated Management at Fisheries and Oceans Canada

Jake Rice National Senior Ecosystem Science Advisor
Fisheries and Oceans Canada, Ottawa, ON

INTRODUCTION

The following three innovations for managing human activities in marine ecosystems are mandated in the preamble to Canada's *Oceans Act*: application of an ecosystem approach, the precautionary approach, and integrated management. Fulfilling these mandates is incremental rather than precipitous, and implementation has to balance accommodating real regional differences in needs and capacities with ensuring consistency in interpreting and applying policies and practices. Cooperation from other government agencies and departments federally, provincially, and municipally is also required. Implementation is far from complete, but major benchmarks have been achieved in both the Science and the Oceans and Habitats sectors of Fisheries and Oceans Canada (DFO). The four phases of implementation are described below.

PHASE 1

Early in the process, DFO recognized the advantages of having management build around explicit ecosystem objectives. A working group on ecosystem objectives, co-chaired by the directors of the Science and the Oceans and Habitats sectors with membership from every region and sector, was launched to identify a framework of ecosystem objectives for implementing an ecosystem approach. The working group organized a major national workshop with international and academic participation in 2001 that produced the following concrete achievements:

- Recognition that ecosystem objectives existed at several levels of specificity, and that planning had to work from general conceptual levels down to explicit operational ones.

- Consensus on a set of overarching conceptual ecosystem objectives, specifically:

  – To conserve enough components (that is, species, populations, etc.) to maintain the natural resilience of the ecosystem.

  – To conserve each component of the ecosystem so that it can play its historic role in the food web.

  – To conserve the physical and chemical properties of the ecosystem.

- Agreement that to be operational an ecosystem objective had to be specific enough to give guidance on a suitable indicator to measure status relative to the objective, and to specify points of reference for limits where functional changes could be observed.

- Acknowledgment of the need for the engagement of stakeholders and academic experts through the entire process of developing and implementing an ecosystem approach and integrated management.

The workshop also focused on the ecosystem approach component of the preamble to the *Oceans Act*, and unfortunately gave comparatively little attention to the integrated management component. This has resulted in lingering differences of view across the country regarding a separate industry sector interpretation of how to implement an ecosystem approach, compared to implementation of integrated management of human activities in the sea within an ecosystem context.

PHASE 2

Following the 2001 workshop and while building on a funding initiative referred to as the Oceans Action

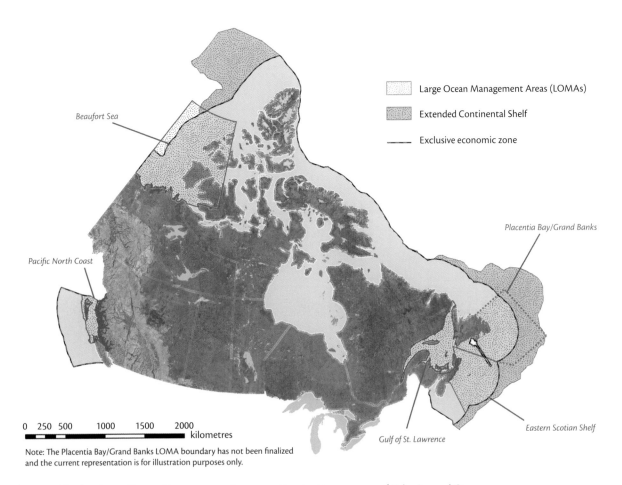

Large Ocean Management Areas (LOMAs)

Extended Continental Shelf

Exclusive economic zone

Beaufort Sea

Placentia Bay/Grand Banks

Pacific North Coast

Eastern Scotian Shelf

0   250 500   1000   1500   2000
                                kilometres

Gulf of St. Lawrence

Note: The Placentia Bay/Grand Banks LOMA boundary has not been finalized
and the current representation is for illustration purposes only.

Figure 1. The five Large Ocean Management Areas used by the Department of Fisheries and Oceans.

Plan (OAP), the Ecosystem Objectives Working Group developed a plan to advance Canada's implementation of the ecosystem approach and integrated management. The DFO Management Committee approved the plan in 2003.

A key initiative of the OAP was the identification of five Large Ocean Management Areas (LOMAs) (Figure 1). These LOMAs, covering Canada's three coasts and oceans, differed in ecological characteristics, the extent and time series of science information available, and the nature of governance and management decision-making. However, all were of a geographic scale and degree of ecological and socioeconomic homogeneity that made each unit suitable for assessing progress toward ecosystem objectives and integrated management planning.

The OAP outlined a sequence of activities for setting conservation, social, and economic objectives for each LOMA to complete by spring 2007. The interdependencies of these activities are illustrated in Figure 2.

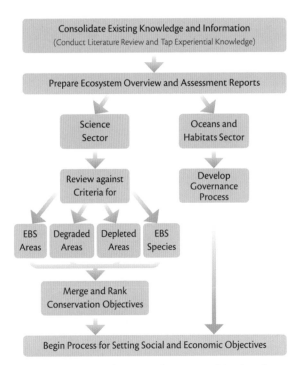

Figure 2. Sequence of activities for setting objectives for the Large Ocean Management Areas. EBS: ecologically or biologically significant.

Each LOMA had to produce an ecosystem overview and an ecosystem assessment with an ecological component covering physical, chemical, and biological information; an anthropogenic component covering social, economic, and cultural activities; and a component covering the nature of the governance processes in the LOMA. The Science sector had the lead in preparing the ecosystem overviews and ecosystem assessments with significant engagement by the Oceans and Habitats sector. The latter led the preparation of the social, economic, cultural, and governance components of the documents.

The ecosystem overview was initially conceived as a comprehensive but descriptive summary of all available information on the LOMA. The ecosystem assessment was to be the integrative component of the documentation, highlighting the important physical and chemical factors driving the biological dynamics, the important species interactions, and the key ways that human activities served as pressures in the ecological processes and structural features. Reflecting differences in regional capacities, the five LOMAs undertook preparation of the ecosystem overviews and assessments in different ways. In some cases, the entire tasks (or at least all but the final stages) were contracted out. In some cases, specific positions within DFO (in the Science and Oceans and Habitats sectors) were created to prepare the documents, pulling together information from experts throughout the department, regional academic centers, environmental non-governmental organizations, and industry. In some cases, Science and Oceans and Habitats management sectors' coordinators were appointed but preparation of the ecosystem overview and ecosystem assessment sections were intended to be collaborative activities, with active engagement from experts throughout the department.

Efforts to complete encyclopaedic overviews were quickly abandoned as a waste of time and effort, replaced by living metadata guides to finding information of various types, and descriptions of how extensive the specific information was. Despite the fact that input from experts not directly assigned to the project was weaker than hoped for, all of the Ecosystem Overview and Assessment Reports (EOAR) were completed by their deadlines. The reports were subjected to an appropriate form of peer review, taking into account the relative balances of experiential knowledge, original analysis and modeling, and summary and synthesis of previously published material. In all cases, the socioeconomic components of the EOARs lagged behind the ecological components, and in most cases were substantially less complete and less quantitative.

PHASE 3

Plans for unpacking the operational ecosystem objectives for each LOMA were developed as the EOARs were being prepared. Although substantial dialogue was required to get all five LOMAs working groups to understand and agree on the relations between the conservation and the social and economic objectives, a national model was developed based on the following specifications:

- Conservation objectives are determined by the structural and functional characteristics of the ecosystem. They are intended to ensure that the consequences of the human activities being managed do not cause serious or irreversible harm to ecosystem structure and function.

- Conservation objectives provide the basis for specifying points of reference for limits (limit reference points) where functional changes in the ecosystem could be observed.

- Because they are based on the ecosystem properties of each LOMA, the best science information (including experiential knowledge) available, and a rigorous peer review process, the Science sector has the lead in determining what conservation objectives are needed for each LOMA.

- Social and economic objectives are determined by the aspirations of the residents of the LOMA, and the policies of the governments. They are intended to specify the nature of the benefits society expects from the LOMA and may reflect social, economic, subsistence, cultural, and aesthetic values.

- Social and economic objectives are the source of target reference points for the indicators associated with the specific objectives.

- Social and economic objectives are set by a consultative process among all levels of government, industries, communities, and stakeholder groups. They are set by a process of negotiation and compromise, facilitated by the Oceans and Habitats sector.

As the processes for setting all of the ecosystem objectives progressed, it became clear that although the Oceans and Habitats sector leads in facilitating establishment of social and economic objectives, the Science sector had two central roles in informing the dialogue leading to their selection. The first was to provide advice on the state of the ecosystem needed to achieve the social and economic objective. The participants in the process of negotiation and compromise leading to the final social and economic objectives might choose to adjust their expectations and goals based on that advice, rather than pay the transition cost of rebuilding the ecosystem components to a state necessary to provide all their aspirational goals. A second and more critical role for Science was to ensure that when considered together, the suite of social and economic objectives could be achievable without violating the conservation objectives. Consequently, the conservation objectives had to be set before the dialogue on social and economic objectives had progressed too far. These conservation objectives served as boundary conditions constraining the consultation and negotiation to allow consideration of only social and economic objectives whose achievement (individually and collectively) did not violate the conservation objectives.

The work in Phase 1 indicated that the three overarching conceptual ecosystem objectives could be unpacked into hundreds, possibly thousands, of very specific conservation objectives. Such lengthy lists of conservation objectives would exceed the capacity of the science community to monitor and evaluate progress, and the capacity of managers to focus on them in management plans and policies. Hence there was a need to make the list short and practical. At the same time, however, these conservation objectives are meant to provide the foundation for protection of ecosystem structure and function. Thus the list needs to be adequate to provide a high level of confidence to the assessment of whether or not the ecosystem structure and function are conserved.

Criteria for identifying areas as ecologically or biologically significant (CSAS 2004)

There are three main dimensions along which specific areas can be evaluated regarding their ecological and biological significance. Interpretation of specific cases on these three dimensions should take account of two additional dimensions on which specific areas can be evaluated.

The main dimensions are continua of

a. Uniqueness—Areas ranked according to characteristics that are unique, rare, distinct, and for which alternatives do not exist elsewhere. Uniqueness may be considered in regional, national, and global context, with increased importance at each scale.

b. Aggregation—Ranked from areas where

i. most individuals of a species are aggregated for some part of the year; OR

ii. most individuals use the area for some important function in their life history; OR

iii. some structural feature or ecological process occurs with exceptionally high density to areas where

- individuals of a species are widespread and even areas of comparatively high density do not contain a substantial portion of the total population; OR

- individuals may congregate to perform a life-history function, but the area in which they perform the function varies substantially over time; OR

- structural property or ecological process occurs in many alternative areas.

c. Fitness consequences—Ranked from areas where the life-history activity(ies) undertaken make a major contribution to the fitness of the population or species present to areas where the life-history activity(ies) undertaken make only marginal contributions to fitness. (This dimension generally applies to functional properties of areas, and in most cases and/or survival of a species. However, "fitness consequences" is considered to be a more inclusive term, to include cases that may influence survival or reproduction indirectly as well as directly.)

The two additional dimensions to be considered when evaluating sites on the three major dimensions are

a. Resilience—from areas where the habitat structures or species are highly sensitive, easily perturbed, and slow to recover to areas where the habitat structures or species are robust, resistant to perturbation, or readily return to the pre-perturbation state. (This dimension more readily applies to structural properties of habitats and ecological communities but can apply to functional properties of species as well.)

b. Naturalness—from areas that are pristine and characterized by native species to areas that are highly perturbed by anthropogenic activities and/or with high abundances of introduced or cultured species.

The planning process identified four types of conservation objectives to be derived from the EOARs. These conservation objectives were associated with:

- ecologically or biologically significant areas

- areas that had been degraded to the point where the ecosystem was already at risk of suffering serious or irreversible harm

- ecologically or biologically significant species and community properties

- species whose populations had been depleted to the point where productivity was at risk of having suffered serious or irreversible harm, and recovery was a priority

These objectives consider the places or species most crucial to ecosystem structure and function and the places and species that already are in poor condition, regardless of the origin of the condition.

To ensure consistency in the standards for setting conservation objectives across LOMAs, the planning process recognized that explicit criteria were needed for extracting each class of candidate conservation objectives from the information in the EOARs. National workshops produced a list of specific criteria for Ecologically or Biologically Significant Areas (EBSAs) (see first box) and gave guidance on their application (CSAS 2004) for Ecologically or Biologically Significant Species/Community Properties (EBSSCPs) (see second box and CSAS 2006).

The list of candidate criteria conservation objectives for degraded places included any areas for which a need for rehabilitation had been identified by any level of government through any legally based process. Criteria for species included depleted species (stocks assessed by DFO to be at unacceptable risk of being below a biomass limit reference point) and any species assessed as threatened or endangered by COSEWIC. Applying these criteria or standards provide each LOMA with four lists of candidate conservation objectives. The four lists, developed with consistency in ecological reasoning and common standards of risk aversion, were combined into a short list of conservation objectives, practical

---

Criteria for identifying species or community properties as ecologically significant (CSAS 2006)

The best approach for identifying ecologically significant species on the basis of their **trophic roles** is to assess the interaction strengths of all the species in the food web. However, for almost all aquatic food webs, we cannot directly identify the species with large interaction strengths. Therefore the best science practice for trophic relationships is to focus on key trophic roles. These include

- Forage species;

- Highly influential predators;

- Nutrient importing (and exporting) species;

- Primary production and decomposition are also essential to ecosystem structure and function. However, they may be less useful as criteria for assessing the ecological significance of species, because they are often difficult to associate with individual species. They are often tied to places that meet EBSA criteria, therefore they often receive enhanced protection through spatial management approaches.

Assessment of **structure-providing species** requires assessing quantity of the species present, quality of the structural habitat being provided, and the significance of the structural habitat to the overall ecosystem structure and function.

Management advice is feasible for **community properties above the species level** as well, although with current knowledge few criteria can be made operational for assessing community properties above the species level as ecologically significant. Properties proposed for use now include

- Size-based properties;

- Frequency distribution of abundance and/or biomass across species.

For some types of species the goal may be to deter explosive growth rather than depletion. The two examples that were identified were

- Invasive species;

- Harmful or toxic species.

Two additional factors, rarity and sensitivity/recoverability, affect the application of the preceding criteria and may move a species or community property somewhat higher in priority ranking.

Criteria for ranking conservation priorities across classes of ecologically or biologically significant areas, degraded areas, ecologically significant species or community properties, or depleted species

It is unrealistic to expect to rank all individual species and areas from highest priority to least high priority. However, there should be an attempt in each LOMA to at least identify a top tier of conservation priorities.

Assigning conservation priorities to the highest priority tier would give highest priority to EBSAs that

- have ecological rationales that are similar to rationales of some species or areas identified as ecologically significant species, depleted or rare species, or degraded areas from the same LOMA, and/or

- are significant to several ecological layers, and/or

- meet several EBSA criteria.

If some key species or community properties that **regulate** ecosystem function are not adequately covered by the highest tier priority EBSAs, then add the necessary ESSs or ESCPs to the tier of highest conservation priorities.

Depleted species should also be in the top tier of conservation priorities where there is an assessed risk of extinction, or the species is below a conservation reference point, and either

- their numbers have been greatly reduced from previous levels or

- they are uncommon species overall **and** are not very widespread.

for planning and management that also considers the conservation needs of all the most important places, species, and community properties (see third box and CSAS 2007). A flow chart for the whole process is presented in Figure 2.

PHASE 4

A major workshop planned for late 2007 will evaluate the approaches taken in each LOMA to identify the best practices for preparing future EOARs and to revise, as necessary, guidelines for the classes of conservation objectives. The progress to date includes completion and peer review of the EOARs for all five of the LOMAs, although social, economic, and governance sections are incomplete in some cases. For all the LOMAS, the four lists of candidate conservation objectives have been combined and prioritized according to the guidelines. Following this workshop, the Science sector will begin identifying indicators and reference points to make each conservation objective operational. A departmental Working Group on Ecosystem Indicators with members from all DFO sectors and regions and chaired by Science has been struck to coordinate this work.

While the Science-led process to identify the conservation objectives has been underway, Oceans and Habitats management has been setting up the governance systems in the LOMAs to establish the fora to conduct the dialogue on social and economic objectives. These integrated management (IM) tables have not been easy

to establish, because DFO can only facilitate the setting of social and economic objectives. All steps involve meeting with other federal departments with management responsibilities for some sectors that use the sea, with provinces and Aboriginal groups, other sea-associated communities, industries, and stakeholder groups. Although the detailed structures of the IM tables are not yet fully defined for any LOMA, the availability of conservation objectives will allow these aspects of the IM process to move forward.

Overall, much remains to be done before DFO and Canada enjoy the full benefits of integrated management within an ecosystem approach, as envisioned in the preamble to the *Oceans Act*. The path that led us to where we are today has not been completely smooth and it included surprises, some pleasant, some less so. Nonetheless, stepping back three years into this initiative, most of us are very impressed by what did get accomplished, progressing from the idea to the currently available products in such a comparatively short time.

SUMMARY OF LESSONS LEARNED

1. It **is** possible to make meaningful progress toward the science basis for integrated management using an ecosystem approach.

2. Extensive ecosystem overview reports are time- and resource-consuming to prepare and are obsolete

almost before they are done. It is much wiser to invest time preparing living documents that are basically metadata with electronic pointers to geo-referenced data sets and publications.

3. Scientific generalists are excellent at coordinating these activities, but engagement of disciplinary experts in some way is essential to have products that the science community will support and that will inform the setting of ecosystem objectives for the practical development and implementation of management plans in the real world.

4. Progress seems fastest if a relatively small group of people are empowered to keep things moving, but only if it is understood that they are continually drawing on the knowledge and abilities of a much larger group of experts who need to be brought together a few times a year. Trying to do everything collectively is a very slow way to move forward.

5. Experiential knowledge from Aboriginal people, communities, industry, and special interest groups **can** be acquired and combined with "classically scientific" information with substantial benefits for all.

6. All experts are busy all the time. The idea that the tasks of writing and analyses will be done by the best experts is naïve. Most experts are eager to share their information and results and want to see them used in (and hopefully strongly influence) the overview reports, assessments, and objective-setting activities. However, they want to share their information with someone else who will do the writing and preparations for these reports. They will not have the time to do the work themselves.

7. Collective workshop and peer review meetings periodically are essential, and if conducted correctly can be dynamic and excite substantial interest among a wide range of experts to contribute information and results.

8. The development of guidelines and criteria for the process is **essential** for keeping work coordinated, sound, and consistent and is useful for engaging scientists.

9. Many of the participants in the working group meetings need education about objectives and about limit, target, and precautionary reference points. Even slightly different subdisciplines of science have very different ideas and tools, and managers and policy makers have different ideas as well. These differences are a serious impediment to communication (and progress) until they have been discussed. Convergence of views is possible, but there must be time spent getting to the convergence.

10. Prioritizing conservation objectives is difficult, particularly among numerous disciplinary experts, whether other stakeholders are present or not. A healthy presence of ecological generalists is very valuable at this step.

11. Many industry stakeholders get very uncomfortable with the notion of challenging conservation objectives. Many non-governmental organization stakeholders get very excited about the notion of challenging conservation objectives. Meetings including both perspectives can be successful, but only if the dialogue stays focused on the ecological information and identifying the needs of the ecosystem.

REFERENCES

[CSAS] Canadian Science Advisory Secretariat. 2004. Identification of ecologically and biologically significant areas. Ecosystem Status Report 2004/006. http://www.dfo-mpo.gc.ca/csas/Csas/status/2004/ESR2004_006_e.pdf [Accessed January 2008.]

[CSAS] Canadian Science Advisory Secretariat. 2006. Identification of ecologically significant species and community properties. CSAS Science Advisory Report 2006/041. http://www.dfo-mpo.gc.ca/csas/Csas/status/2006/SAR-AS2006_041_E.pdf [Accessed January 2008.]

[CSAS] Canadian Science Advisory Secretariat. 2007. Guidance document on identifying conservation priorities and phrasing conservation objectives for Large Ocean Management Areas. CSAS Science Advisory Report 2007/10. http://www.dfo-mpo.gc.ca/csas/Csas/status/2007/SAR-AS2007_010_E.pdf [Accessed January 2008.]

Conclusions

Conclusions

Brenda McAfee Acting Director, Forest Science Division
Canadian Forest Service, Natural Resources Canada, Ottawa, ON

Christian Malouin Forest Biological Resources Analyst, Forest Science Division
Canadian Forest Service, Natural Resources Canada, Ottawa, ON

INTRODUCTION

Canada's forests, covering an area equivalent to more than five times the size of Finland and Sweden combined, represent 10% of the world's forests. These dynamic ecosystems provide critical regulating services for climate, air, and water and support a natural resources industry contributing 13% to the country's gross domestic product (NRCan 2005) and to the well-being of a vast number of Canadians. The challenging task of managing forests to maintain sustainable flows of these ecosystem services has been the focus of on-going discussion over the past few decades. In May 2007, it was also the theme of a Science-Policy Dialogue organized by Natural Resources Canada and Environment Canada. This paper provides an overview of the extent and status of ecosystem-based management in Canada's forests based on the papers presented at this workshop or prepared for this publication by experts and practitioners of ecosystem-based management.

In his welcoming remarks, Jim Farrell, Assistant Deputy Minister, Canadian Forest Service, Natural Resources Canada (NRCan), described how NRCan's vision for integrated decision-making included aligning the country's assets, its people (their knowledge, skills, and ideas), its natural resources (air, water, biodiversity, and natural spaces), and its structure (physical and governance systems) to improve the overall quality of life for Canadians. To realize this vision, NRCan is striving to break institutional barriers by forming new partnerships and facilitating cooperative actions. He congratulated the organizers of the workshop for thinking outside the box and taking the first steps toward integrative actions by initiating a dialogue on ecosystem-based management between two sectors that will be interacting

more closely in future as Canada develops strategies for adapting to changing environmental conditions and mitigating cumulative impacts on forests.

The Directors General from both federal departments emphasized that Canada and the world faced new and multifaceted challenges, such as climate change and loss of biodiversity, and that meeting these challenges required an integrated approach to the management of ecosystems coordinated across jurisdictional boundaries and spatial scales. Dan Wicklum described how Environment Canada was gradually incorporating an ecosystem approach into all of its activities in response to the growing concerns of Canadians about environmental issues. He stressed the need for governments to find innovative ways to conceptualize and manage issues over longer and broader time and spatial scales and to work collaboratively with multiple partners. Geoff Munro (NRCan) reminded participants that managing complex systems (for example, working landscapes) for multiple values was a balancing act that the forest sector has been improving over the past two decades. The Canadian Council of Forest Ministers' Criteria and Indicators of Sustainable Forest Management, its framework for integrating social, ecological, and economic aspects, was designed to evolve with new knowledge and changing social values.

CONCEPTUAL THINKING

Successful implementation of systems approaches to management is based on the recognition that human beings are an intrinsic part of ecosystems. An understanding of the structure and dynamics of these systems is also required. In the "Conceptual Thinking" section of this publication, several authors describe how policy responses to changing values toward threats to the biophysical environment have resulted in the development of holistic frameworks incorporating the concept of ecosystem-based management, both internationally and in Canada. Hendrickson describes the shift to ecosystem-based approaches for sustainable development of fisheries, agriculture, forests, and tourism that occurred in Canada over the past 30 years. Conservation and sustainable use of biodiversity have been common drivers for this shift in all these sectors. The decision by the Convention on Biological Diversity (CBD) to make the ecosystem approach its primary framework for action stimulated research and conceptual thinking on systems planning and management. In his article, Hendrickson points out that rather than "over-conceptualizing" the approach, what is now needed is to focus on lessons learned from case studies to extend implementation. The Biodiversity Outcomes Framework, adopted by the Canadian Councils of Resource Ministers in 2006, provides an opportunity for sectors to develop their biodiversity objectives as a contribution toward a national ecosystem-based approach for implementation of the Canadian Biodiversity Strategy.

Harris identifies the urgent need for science, at broad spatial and temporal scales, to increase understanding of ecosystem structures and processes and the influence of human-induced actions on them. He describes how decision-making at multiple scales is restrained by the lack of readily accessible information on the status and trends of ecosystems and further identifies a coordinated monitoring network as a capacity gap. His vision for a national ecosystem approach to environmental management includes a coordinating mechanism for science, the creation of enabling institutions and processes, and facilitated implementation through effective programs at multiple scales.

In his paper, Andrews echoes the need for national coordination and describes how the groundwork conducted by the Canadian Coalition for Integrated Landscape Management provides a starting point. He suggests that a center of excellence to address land use and resource management issues can provide the impetus required to enhance national implementation and increase synergy between science and policy issues.

The *Species at Risk Act* and the *Oceans Act* both embed ecosystem-based management, and their implementation

has enhanced understanding of the concept. The maintenance and recovery of healthy populations of species at risk is a shared federal, provincial, and territorial responsibility where recovery plans have traditionally focused on individual species. Providing some examples of synergy between the *Species at Risk Act* and the *Oceans Act*, Fowler pointed out that a multispecies or ecosystem approach to species at risk would be a cost-effective way to recover species and a be model for integrating management activities from governments, industries, and non-governmental organizations, across sectors and jurisdictions.

Rice describes the process that Fisheries and Oceans Canada used to establish an ecosystem approach for implementing the *Oceans Act*. He highlights the need for scientific rigour, effective science and policy interplay throughout the process, national level coordination, and strong regional/provincial/national collaboration as keys to success.

TOOLS FOR DEVELOPING ECOSYSTEM-BASED APPROACHES

Increased understanding of complex systems, prediction of management effects, and decision-making on future scenarios have been greatly facilitated by an array of existing tools. Such tools include schemes for ecological classification, ecological and landscape models to understand ecosystem dynamics and forecast responses to management scenarios, visualization programs, or information systems providing access to baseline data. Providing baseline data for scientists or synthesized information for community participation or legislative decision-making, these tools integrate science and policy at the management interface. Cutko et al. demonstrate how NatureServe Vista can be used to evaluate scenarios for various land uses and to monitor their impact on management objectives. Although development of ecosystem management tools has focused primarily on ecological factors such as natural disturbance regimes, integrated models are now simulating ecological consequences linked to environmental or policy changes. There is also progress in attempts to establish a common currency to compare natural resources and environmental services. Patriquin and Adamowicz illustrate how such models improve understanding of the economic consequences of alternative actions in the Foothills Model Forest in Alberta, while Hearn et al.

developed a risk assessment framework to integrate a suite of ecological and socioeconomic models.

RECENT EFFORTS, EXPERIMENTS, AND LESSONS LEARNED

Although a well-defined nation-wide approach for systems-based management may not exist, numerous discussions at multiple fora have taken place, a wealth of definitions, principles, criteria, and guidelines exist, and many case studies have been established from which lessons can be learned. In recent years, subnational management authorities have adopted the concept and are currently active in filling the gaps and extending implementation across forested landscapes. The highlights of some of these case studies follow.

Rice and Man describe implementation of the Ontario policy framework for ecological and sustainable management of forest resources at the operational level. The Stand Level Adaptive Management (SLAM) Mixedwood Project respects the vast majority of the relevant ecosystem approach principles developed by the CBD. Allowing practitioners to develop sound management practices adapted to the aspen-dominated mixedwood ecosystem in northern Ontario, SLAM provides a particularly interesting operational application of principle 4—the need to understand and manage the ecosystem in an economic context. Alternative silvicultural treatments are tested with duel objectives to regenerate productive commercial stands and to maintain ecological integrity. The key factors attributed to the success of this initiative are a well-developed framework for active adaptive management; support from a broad group of stakeholders; and the collaboration of Lake Abitibi Model Forest, a one-stop organization for reaching out to forest stakeholders and local communities.

In an in-depth review of the application of the ecosystem approach (CBD 2007), the CBD reported that although current global experience and guidance applies largely at the local site-specific level (where communities can participate more directly), the uptake by national, regional, and local governmental planning processes is slow. The development of institutions to address both environmental protection and improvement of human welfare was recommended as a means to facilitate and accelerate the implementation process. In his paper, Seiferling describes how the province of Alberta, facing growing and cumulative pressures on its land base, is responding to the CBD's recommendation by implementing Sustainable Resource and Environmental Management (SREM). This approach to management is a way of thinking and acting, working collaboratively, and taking joint responsibility for achieving agreed-upon natural resource and environmental outcomes (Alberta Government 2006). It also relies on the development of performance measures, another key issue identified by the CBD review (CBD 2007). SREM recognizes that issues related to natural resources, environment, biodiversity, water quality, and other land uses must be managed through an integrated set of policies to minimize cumulative impacts. The strategic systems approach developed to implement SREM follows adaptive management principles and relies on shared information systems. With the Alberta Biodiversity Monitoring Institute to follow management impacts on biodiversity, Alberta is making significant progress toward a province-wide ecosystem approach.

British Columbia, where the forest industry is an important contributor to its economy, has also undertaken the transition toward an ecosystem-based approach to land-use management by designating Land and Resource Management Planning areas. MacKinnon discusses how the concept has been implemented within two of these areas, the Central and the North Coast Land and Resource Management Planning areas. In each area, the planning involves collaboration across multiple scales and is based on adaptive management. An assessment of risk associated with management actions appears to be particular to the province. Acceptable levels of risk are set according to local conditions and landscapes (for example, range of natural variability). MacKinnon emphasized the need for improved integration of socio-economic and ecological objectives.

With the longest history in forest harvesting in Canada, some Maritime provinces have also taken significant steps toward integrated ecosystem-based management. Stewart and Neily describe how Nova Scotia's integrated resources management system relies on a well-developed ecological land classification, integration of multiple values through public and stakeholder consultations, development of landscape analysis tools, and multi-scale complementary policies extending across provincial legislation and forest certification schemes. New Brunswick has taken a similar route with a hierarchical planning framework for sustainable forest management allowing management objectives to be defined at scales appropriate for ecological processes (for example, habitat, old-growth) as well as socioeconomic aspects (for example, wood supply).

In addition to the individual case studies described in the chapters of this publication, Canadian examples of management systems incorporating the ecosystem approach principles (outlined by Hendrickson) or demonstrating the common elements of holistic approaches to planning and managing human activities outlined in the Introduction were identified. These case studies, illustrating the wealth of experiences across the country, are compiled in Appendix 2. This compilation, produced by consultation of governmental Web sites and information exchange with key experts, includes the following information (if available) for each site:

1. name of policy or program framed by principles of integrated ecosystem-based management of the area;

2. name of the body or mechanism allowing for science input in the planning and adaptive management processes;

3. name of the institutional entity or structure created to implement the management plan;

4. concise description of the case study, emphasizing any unique aspects; and

5. authoritative reference(s) available on the internet.

An analysis of the case studies using these criteria resulted in the following observations:

- **Integrated ecosystem-based management principles are entrenched in federal, provincial, and territorial legislation frameworks.** These jurisdictions have taken decisive steps to enforce implementation by embedding ecosystem-based management principles into policies for natural resources, wildlife, species at risk, parks, land use, or First Nations.

- **Policies and enabling organizations are being created to make implementation of ecosystem-based management possible at appropriate scales.** In most of the case studies, governance is through an established responsible organization or institutional body, having a clear mandate, management authority, appropriate structure, and sufficient (or access to)

scientific and technical means. Depending on the size of the management area, these organizations are either governmental, operating at arm's length from government, or independent. When part of government departments (typical for provincial or large management areas), ecosystem values (ecological and socioeconomic) are determined through consultation with stakeholders, but decisions are made by the responsible department(s). In addition to establishing appropriate management structures, jurisdictions are starting to create linkages between existing policies to develop a systems-focused policy framework to replace the "silo" approach where numerous independent policies covered the same landscape. Alberta's Sustainable Resource and Environmental Management policy is a good example of this trend. Arm's length organizations, mandated by legislation to develop and implement management plans, may also consult with local stakeholder groups. Independent organizations typically develop and implement ecosystem-based management on private lands or as part of a company's stewardship agenda.

- **Model Forests and Biosphere Reserves were incubators and in situ laboratories for broader adoption of ecosystem-based management and continue to play an important role in advancing the concept.** Canada's Model Forests and Biosphere Reserves, supported by extensive networks of local, national, and international partnerships, have contributed hands-on experience and increased capacity for implementation of integrated ecosystem-based management.

- **Co-management arrangements between First Nations and provincial or federal governments, framed around an ecosystem approach, have been incorporated into settlement of some land claims issues.** In several case studies, the guiding principles of ecosystem-based management encouraging mutual respect, collaboration to achieve shared outcomes, and incorporation of indigenous and local knowledge and practices appear to have facilitated co-management agreements.

- **Organizations responsible for management have established or are associated with a clearly mandated scientific body.** In most of the case studies examined, management authorities rely on a scientific or technical advisory body to provide science input for decision-making processes and develop tools to assist with planning, monitoring, and reporting.

- **Implementation of ecosystem-based management has been driven primarily by local processes.** Consistent with principle 2 of the ecosystem approach, which suggests that management should be decentralized to the lowest appropriate level, implementation of ecosystem-based management has been driven from the bottom up through community groups or non-governmental agencies. Increasingly, government agencies (often natural resources departments) are turning to these processes to meet multiple policy goals. Examples of several innovative provincial initiatives are included in this publication.

- **The absence of adequate monitoring is an obstacle to implementation of ecosystem-based management.** Providing feedback on the outcomes of management decisions on the landscape, monitoring is a key process in ecosystem-based management. Monitoring systems across the country are not harmonized or well coordinated and, in some cases, are not available at an appropriate scale to answer management questions. Integrated monitoring programs, now being tested, may soon be able to provide examples of best practices to address this gap.

- **Certified forests are important components of Canada's overall framework for achieving integrated ecosystem-based management.** Although not included as part of the case studies compiled in Appendix 2, third-party certification standards for sustainable forest management (for example, Canadian Standards Association, Forest Stewardship Council, Sustainable Forestry Initiative) are important drivers for adoption of ecosystem-based guidelines for planning and managing land-use activities in forests. More than 90% of the land allotted for operational forestry in Canada is certified under one or more of these standards (Canadian Sustainable Forestry Certification Coalition 2007). Based on adaptive management and continuous improvement in overall effectiveness at meeting desired outcomes, certified forest areas are important management unit level contributions to implementation of ecosystem-based management across the landscape.

SUMMARY OF PROGRESS

Responding to the request from the CBD Secretariat for member Parties to share case studies that demonstrate the benefits of using the ecosystem approach to achieve biodiversity-related global objectives (SCBD 2007), this publication provides a preliminary portrait of the configurations and extent of implementation of ecosystem approaches in Canada. Discussions at the Science-Policy Dialogue in May 2007, and the follow-up activities, provided input to the 12th meeting of the CBD's Subsidiary Body on Scientific, Technical and Technological Advice (SBSTTA) and will also contribute to discussions at the 9th Conference of the Parties in May 2008. In his paper, Hendrickson recalls the message from SBSTTA 12 that "full application of the (ecosystem) approach in all of its ecological, social, economic, cultural, and political dimensions remains a formidable task, particularly at the larger scale".

A review of the case studies included in this publication indicates that Canada has made significant progress in advancing the ecosystem approach concept in forest ecosystems. Integrated ecosystem-based approaches to sustainable development and land and resource management have gained broad acceptance at multiple levels of application in Canada. Examples of systems approaches to managing human activities in forests occur in all jurisdictions. The forest sector has been a driving force in the development of ecosystem-based management and a pioneer in its implementation. Criteria and indicators of sustainable forest management and certification standards provide ecosystem-based management frameworks that accommodate multisector activities. Provincial forest management plans serve as mechanisms for integrating planning of multiple forest uses. Conservation and species at risk are routine considerations in these plans, while tourism, recreation, other industrial activities, and environmental assessment have been integrated to varying degrees. Model forests with their wide and varied network of partnerships are epicenters for extending the adoption of ecosystem-based management. As a result, an increasingly large total forest area in Canada is managed under ecosystem-based management plans with clear objectives for respecting the multiple values attached to the landscape, maintaining sustainable flows of natural resources, and assessing and managing risk associated with cumulative impacts.

REFERENCES

Alberta Government. 2006. Sustainable Resource and Environmental Management (SREM). http://www.srem.gov.ab.ca [Accessed March 2008.]

Canadian Sustainable Forestry Certification Coalition. 2007. Certification status—June 2007. http://www.certification canada.org/english/status_intentions/status.php [Accessed March 2008.]

[CBD] Convention on Biological Diversity. 2007. In-depth review of the application of the ecosystem approach—Note by the Executive Secretary. www.cbd.int/doc/meetings/sbstta/sbstta-12/official/sbstta-12-02-en.pdf [Accessed March 2008.]

[NRCan] Natural Resources Canada. 2005. Statistics on natural resources. http://www.nrcan.gc.ca/statistics/factsheet.htm [Accessed March 2008.]

[SCBD] Secretariat of the Convention on Biological Diversity. 2007. Notification re: Submission of further case studies on the Ecosystem Approach for the Ecosystem Approach Sourcebook. http://www.cbd.int/doc/notifications/ 2007/ntf-2007-084-ea-en.pdf [Accessed March 2008.]

Appendices

 # Appendix 1

"Sectors across Forested Landscapes: Sustainable Systems through Integration and Innovation"

NATURAL RESOURCES CANADA, CAMSELL HALL, 580 BOOTH STREET, OTTAWA
MAY 24–25, 2007

Workshop Agenda

OBJECTIVES

- To share knowledge on best-management practices contributing to the implementation of the ecosystem approach in Canada's forests.

- To stimulate the integration of best-management practices across sectors and scales.

- To develop input for Canada's position at the 12th meeting of the Subsidiary Body on Scientific, Technical, and Technological Advice of the Convention on Biological Diversity.

ROAD MAP

Day 1—May 24, 2007

08:00   Beverages, registration

A. Introduction and Context

08:30   Welcoming Remarks .... **Jim Farrell, ADM, Natural Resources Canada**

08:35   Introduction to Science-Policy Dialogue .... **Geoff Munro, Natural Resources Canada, Dan Wicklum, Environment Canada**

08:50   Framing the Workshop
- Desired outcomes .... **Brenda McAfee, Natural Resources Canada, Canadian Forest Service**

09:00   Agenda Review
- Introductions, how we will work together .... **Facilitator**

09:10   Open Forum—Q&A

B. Conceptual Thinking on Ecosystem Approaches

(15-min presentations followed by 5-min Q&A session each)

09:20   Why the Ecosystem Approach and Why Now .... **Ken Harris, Environment Canada**

09:40   The Convention on Biological Diversity and the Ecosystem Approach .... **Ole Hendrickson, Environment Canada**

10:00   An Ecosystem Approach for Species at Risk .... **Tom J. Fowler, Fisheries and Oceans Canada**

10:20   Health Break

10:40   Discussion : **A common understanding for systems approaches in Canada**
- What are some of the main elements characterizing systems approaches to landscape management in Canada?
- How do Canadian approaches compare with the ecosystem approach of the Convention on Biological Diversity?

C. Key Recent Efforts, Experiments, and Lessons in Developing Ecosystem Approaches

(15-min presentations followed by 5-min Q&A session each)

11:30   Alberta Land-Use Framework .... **Morris Seiferling, ADM, Sustainable Resource and Environmental Management, Alberta**

11:50   Lessons from the Great Bear Rainforest .... **Andy MacKinnon, British Columbia Ministry of Forests and Range**

12:30   Lunch

13:30   Discussion: **Implementing systems approaches in Canada**
- What are the key challenges/barriers (knowledge, decision-making, action) to implementing the ecosystem approach?

14:15   The Stand Level Adaptive Management
Mixedwood Research Project .... **James A. Rice, Ontario Ministry of Natural Resources**

14:35   NatureServe Vista: A Decision-Support Tool for Forest
and Conservation Planning .... **Andy Cutko, NatureServe**

15:00   Health Break

15:15   Discussion: **Implementing systems approaches in Canada** *(Continued)*
- Are there additional challenges to add to the list?
- What are the key lessons learned from these case studies with respect to knowledge, decision-making, and integrated action?

16:25   Wrap-up .... **Facilitator**

16:30   End Day 1

Day 2—May 25, 2007

08:00   Beverages

08:30   Getting Started
- Agenda review
- Synthesis of key messages from Day 1 .... **Facilitator**

08:45   Discussion
- Have we got it right?
- Anything to add? .... **Facilitator**

D. Solutions and Progress

(15-min presentations followed by 5-min Q&A session each)

09:30   Integrated Risk Analysis Framework .... **Brian J. Hearn, David R. Gray, Joan E. Luther,**
Natural Resources Canada, Canadian Forest Service

09:50   Integrative Perspectives on Alternate Landscapes Futures .... **Kathryn Lindsay, Environment Canada**

10:10   Modeling Natural Resources Management Policies
in the Foothills Model Forest .... **Mike N. Patriquin, Natural Resources Canada,**
Canadian Forest Service

10:30   Health Break

10:45   Discussion: **Identifying innovative solutions**
- What tools or processes could be used to overcome implementation challenges?
- Are there current opportunities for testing some of the proposed solutions?

12:00   Lunch

13:00   Options for facilitating the implementation of ecosystem
approaches in Canada .... **Dan Wicklum, Environment Canada**
Geoff Munro, Natural Resources Canada

13:20   Discussion: **Moving forward**
- What are other options?
- Which one is most practical/realistic?

14:30   Wrap-up
- Next steps .... **Brenda McAfee, Natural Resources Canada, Canadian Forest Service**

15:00   Workshop Close

Participants

Candace Anderson
Canadian Environmental Assessment Agency

Stephan Barg
International Institute for Sustainable Development

Aomar Boukhezar
International Consultant

Catherine Carmody
Natural Resources Canada
Canadian Forest Service

Michel Charron
Natural Resources Canada
Canadian Forest Service

Martha Copestake
Eastern Ontario Model Forest

Steve Curtis
Agriculture and Agri-Food Canada

Andy Cutko
NatureServe

Henry C. de Gooijer
Agriculture and Agri-Food Canada

Nicole De Silva
Natural Resources Canada
Canadian Forest Service

Rhian Evans
Natural Resources Canada
GeoConnections

Jim Farrell
Natural Resources Canada
Canadian Forest Service

Tom J. Fowler
Fisheries and Oceans Canada

Steve Gordon
New Brunswick Department of Natural Resources

Andrea Grant
Natural Resources Canada
Canadian Forest Service

David R. Gray
Natural Resources Canada
Canadian Forest Service
Atlantic Forestry Centre

John Hall
Natural Resources Canada
Canadian Forest Service

Ken Harris
Environment Canada

Ole Hendrickson
Environment Canada

Nancy Hofmann
Statistics Canada

Paula Irving
Natural Resources Canada
Canadian Forest Service

Bonnie James
Environment Canada

Jean-Pierre Jetté
Ministère des Ressources naturelles et de la Faune
Quebec

Judith Kennedy
Environment Canada

Louise Kingsley
Environment Canada

Jan Klimaszewski
Natural Resources Canada
Canadian Forest Service
Laurentian Forestry Centre

Elsie Krebs
Environment Canada

Hélène Lévesque
Environment Canada

Kathryn Lindsay
Environment Canada

Joan E. Luther
Natural Resources Canada
Canadian Forest Service
Atlantic Forestry Centre

Andy MacKinnon
British Columbia Ministry of Forests and Range

Christian Malouin
Natural Resources Canada
Canadian Forest Service

Brenda McAfee
Natural Resources Canada
Canadian Forest Service

Robert McFetridge
Federal Biodiversity Information Partnership

Don McNicol
Canadian Wildlife Service

Rick Moll
Statistics Canada

Geoff Munro
Natural Resources Canada
Canadian Forest Service

Erin Neave
Wren Resources

David Neave
Wren Resources

Cathy Nielsen
Environment Canada

Holly Palen
Natural Resources Canada
Canadian Forest Service

Mike N. Patriquin
Natural Resources Canada
Canadian Forest Service
Northern Forestry Centre

James A. Rice
Ontario Ministry of Natural Resources

Morris Seiferling
Sustainable Resource and Environmental Management
Government of Alberta

Wendy Vasbinder
Natural Resources Canada
Canadian Forest Service

Stephen Virc
Environment Canada

Jan Volney
Natural Resources Canada
Canadian Forest Service
Northern Forestry Centre

Dan Wicklum
Environment Canada

Warren Wilson
The Intersol Group

Appendix 2

Canadian Case Studies Illustrating the Convention on Biological Diversity's Ecosystem Approach Principles

Case Studies	Supporting Policies and Programs	Supporting Science Body or Programs	Enabling Organization	Description
ALBERTA				
Land-use Framework (for public and private lands in the province) **Area:** not available http://www.srem.gov.ab.ca/ http://www.landuse.gov.ab.ca/ http://www.srd.gov.ab.ca/lands/usingpublicland/integratedland management/default.aspx	Alberta's commitment to Sustainable Resource and Environmental Management (1999) Integrated Land Management Program	Sustainable Resource and Environmental Management Integrated Landscape Management Innovation Network	Sustainable Resource and Environmental Management	See Seiferling (this publication).
Foothills Model Forest (1992) **Area:** 2.75 million ha http://www.modelforest.net/cmfn/en/forests/foothills/default.aspx http://www.fmf.ca/	Model Forest Program (1992)	Various research programs	Foothills Model Forest Board of Directors	The Foothills Model Forest, with two parks and industrial forest management areas, develops projects for 12 program themes. Examples include projects on the impacts of natural disturbances, the monitoring of grizzly bear populations, socio-economic impacts of tourism, watershed planning, water quality, and forest health.
Peace Area **Area:** 9.1 million ha http://www.srd.gov.ab.ca/lands/usingpublicland/integratedlandman agement/pdf/Peace_area_Draft_Terms_of_Reference.pdf	Peace Area Access Management Plan (2005, draft)	Department of Sustainable Resource Development	Department of Sustainable Resource Development	The plan aims to manage land and resource access while reducing human impacts and the fragmentation of habitats.
Beaver Hills Initiative (BHI) (2000) **Area:** 160 000 ha http://www.beaverhills.ab.ca/	N/A	BHI Coordinating Committee	BHI Coordinating Committee	The initiative focuses on the natural beauty and quality of life of the region and supports cooperative efforts to sustain quality of water, land, air, and natural resources and community development. The outcome is provision of information to decision makers.
Northern East Slopes Area **Area:** 7.7 million ha http://www3.gov.ab.ca/env/regions/nes/strategy.html	Northern East Slopes Sustainable Resource and Environmental Management Strategy (1999)	Regional Steering Group	Regional Steering Group	The strategy seeks the integrated management of natural resources to ensure a healthy and sustainable environment, economy, and community that can be enjoyed by present and future generations.

Case Studies	Supporting Policies and Programs	Supporting Science Body or Programs	Enabling Organization	Description
BRITISH COLUMBIA				
Provincial Public Lands http://ilmbwww.gov.bc.ca/lup/	*Forest and Range Practices Act (2004)* Land and Resource Management Planning: A Statement of Principles and Process (1993) Sustainable Resource Management Planning—A Landscape-level Strategy for Resource Development (2002)	Integrated Land Management Bureau	Integrated Land Management Bureau	British Columbia's land base is divided into land-use zones. Subregional land and resource management plans are designed to create a vision for integrated use and management of public provincial lands and resources.
Muskwa-Kechika Management Area (1998) **Area:** 6.4 million ha http://www.muskwa-kechika.com/ http://www.qp.gov.bc.ca/statreg/stat/M/98038_01.htm	*Muska-Kechika Management Area Act (1998)*	Research financially supported through a trust fund Support from local academic institutions	Muskwa-Kechika Advisory Board	One of the largest conservation systems in North America, it comprises parks and protected areas where resource extraction is prohibited, and management zones where resource extraction may occur if best management practices are followed. Management standards are higher than elsewhere in the province.
Clayoquot Sound Area, a UNESCO Biosphere Reserve (2000) **Area:** 262 600 ha http://www.nrtee.ca/eng/publications/case-studies/natural-heritage/eng/clayoquot-case-study-Full-Report-eng.html http://srmwww.gov.bc.ca/rmd/specialprojects/clayquot/ http://www.clayoquotbiosphere.org/ http://www.centralregionboard.com/index.html	Interim Measures Extension Agreement: A Bridge to Treaty (1994) Forest Communities Program (2007)	Scientific Panel for Sustainable Forest Practices in Clayoquot Sound (1993)	Central Region Board	Clayoquot Sound area is co-managed by local First Nations and the provincial government. The agreed management approach is based on increasing the amount of protected areas, protecting old-growth forests, and integrating resources management and social stability.
North and Central Coast Planning Area **Area:** 5.6 million ha http://ilmbwww.gov.bc.ca/lup/lrmp/coast/central_north_coast/index.html http://ilmbwww.gov.bc.ca/citbc/	South Central Coast Order (2007) Land Use Objectives Regulation (2005)	Coast Information Team (panel of experts in social, economic, and biological research)	Planning Tables Implementation and Monitoring Committee for each area Ecosystem-based Management Working Group	See MacKinnon (this publication). This case study comprises two land-use zones of British Columbia. The development of ecosystem-based management in these regions has served as a model for other zones in British Columbia.
Sayward Landscape Unit Plan (2003) **Area:** 112 000 ha http://ilmbwww.gov.bc.ca/lup/srmp/coast/campbell_river/index.html http://ilmbwww.gov.bc.ca/lup/srmp/coast/campbell_river/sayward/Saywardlup.pdf	*Forest Practices Code of British Columbia Act (1996)*	District staff of the ministries of Forests and Range, Sustainable Resource Management, and Water, Land and Air Protection	Ministries of Forests and Range, Sustainable Resource Management, and Water, Land and Air Protection	Landscape unit planning was undertaken across the province as part of the *Forest Practices Code of British Columbia Act*. The Sayward plan includes biodiversity, recreation, visual landscape, timber, domestic water, and mineral values.

Case Studies	Supporting Policies and Programs	Supporting Science Body or Programs	Enabling Organization	Description
Horsefly Sustainable Resource Management Plan (SRMP) (2005) **Area:** 813 021 ha http://ilmbwww.gov.bc.ca/lup/srmp/northern/horsefly/index.html http://ilmbwww.gov.bc.ca/lup/srmp/northern/horsefly/Horsefly_SRMP_Final.pdf	Cariboo-Chilcotin Land Use Plan (1994) *Forest Practices Code of British Columbia Act (1996)*	Integrated Land Management Bureau Associates	Integrated Land Management Bureau	This plan provides detailed area-based resource targets and strategies for timber, range, mining, fish, wildlife, biodiversity conservation, water management, tourism, recreation, agriculture, and handcraft/agro-forestry.
Resources North Association (initial phase includes South Peace, Mackenzie, and Vanderhoof–Fort St. James areas) **Area:** not available http://www.modelforest.net/cmfn/en/forests/mcgregor/default.aspx http://www.resourcesnorth.org/rna	Forest Communities Program (2007)	Various research associates	McGregor Model Forest Board of Directors Integrated Resources Management Partnerships	Resources North Association originates from a collaboration between the McGregor Model Forest Association and the Integrated Resource Management Partnership of Northern British Columbia. The goal is to improve the integration of community needs into landscape management.
Mount Robson Provincial Park (1913), a World Heritage Site (1990) **Area:** 223 000 ha http://www.env.gov.bc.ca/bcparks/planning/mgmtplns/mtrobson/mt_robson_draft_mp2007.pdf http://www.env.gov.bc.ca/bcparks/explore/parkpgs/mtrobson.html http://ilmbwww.gov.bc.ca/lup/lrmp/northern/robson/plan/toc.htm http://www.env.gov.bc.ca/bcparks/conserve/occ_paper/mtrobson.html	Management Plan for Mount Robson Provincial Park (2007, under review) Robson Valley Land and Resources Management Plan	Ministry of Environment	Ministry of Environment	The 2007 management plan for the area proposes an interagency approach to ecosystem management, improved information on ecological values and backcountry recreation opportunities, a revised provincial park zoning system, and an increased emphasis on working with and establishing a new relationship with First Nations.
MANITOBA				
Provincial Public Forest Lands http://www.gov.mb.ca/conservation/forestry/forest-practices/planning/fpp-aops.html	Manitoba Forest Plans... Toward Ecosystems Based Management (1996) Manitoba's Provincial Sustainable Development Code of Practice (2001)	Manitoba Conservation	Manitoba Conservation Regional Integrated Resource Management Team	Manitoba has committed to sustainable development and ecosystem-based approaches for forest management.
Manitoba Model Forest (1992) **Area:** 1.05 million ha http://www.modelforest.net/cmfn/en/forests/manitoba/default.aspx http://www.manitobamodelforest.net/	Model Forest Program (1992) Forest Communities Program (2007)	Various research partners	Manitoba Model Forest Board of Directors	The Manitoba Model Forest is developing new partnerships with the forest industry, forest-based communities, and the Assembly of Manitoba Chiefs. The Model Forest is seeking new opportunities for communities to participate in informed decision-making about landscape management and to develop alternative uses of forest resources.

Case Studies	Supporting Policies and Programs	Supporting Science Body or Programs	Enabling Organization	Description
East Side Lake Winnipeg Planning Initiative (Wabanong Nakaygum Okimawin) (2000) **Area:** not available Note: This region includes the Manitoba Model Forest. http://www.gov.mb.ca/conservation/wno/	Canada–Manitoba Partnership Agreement in Forestry "Promises to Keep…" Towards a Broad Area Plan for the East Side of Lake Winnipeg (2004) Agreement between the Wabanong Nakaygum Okimawin First Nation Governments and the Government of Manitoba (2007)	Manitoba Conservation	Manitoba Conservation East Side Round Table First Nations Council	The objective of the east side planning process is to bring together local communities, First Nations, industry, and environmental organizations to develop a vision for land and resource use in the area that respects both the value of the boreal forest and the needs of local communities.
NEW BRUNSWICK				
Provincial Public Forest Lands http://www.gnb.ca/0078/publications/Policy-CLM0132004-E.pdf http://142.139.24.21/e-repository/monographs/30000000043979/30000000043979.pdf	*Crown Lands and Forests Act* (1982) The New Brunswick Public Forest—Our shared future (2005) Objectives and Standards for the New Brunswick Crown Forest for the 2007–2012 Period (2005)	New Brunswick Department of Natural Resources	New Brunswick Department of Natural Resources	See Gordon (this publication).
Fundy Model Forest **Area:** 420 000 ha http://www.fundymodelforest.net/ http://www.modelforest.net/cmfn/en/forests/fundy/default.aspx	Model Forest Program (2002) Forest Communities Program (2007)	Ecological Thresholds and Monitoring Working Group Sustainable Forest Management Working Group	Fundy Model Forest Board of Directors	This model forest aims at achieving, enhancing, restoring, and sustaining a healthy Acadian forest ecosystem by building capacity for sustainable forest management and conservation of natural biodiversity.
Black Brook District **Area:** 190 000 ha http://www.sfmnetwork.ca/html/project_63_e.html http://www.sfmnetwork.ca/html/project_76_e.html http://www.unites.uqam.ca/rlq/colloque2006/presentations/presentation_maclean.pdf http://www.jdirving.com/uploadedFiles/Environment/Research/UniqueAreas.pdf	J.D. Irving Limited's Unique Areas Program	University of New Brunswick	J.D. Irving Limited Forest Research Advisory Committee	This area is private forest land where a triad approach is being implemented. The strategy includes zoning reserves and intensively managed stands within a landscape managed with silviculture inspired by natural disturbance. It aims at protecting all values associated with the landscape.
NEWFOUNDLAND AND LABRADOR				
Provincial Public Forest Lands http://www.nr.gov.nl.ca/forestry/publications/SFM.pdf#xml=http://search.gov.nl.ca/texis/search/pdfhi.txt?query=ecosystem+approach+forests+&pr=provincial&prox=page&rorder=500&rprox=750&rdfreq=250&rwfreq=500&rlead=500&sufs=2&order=r&cq=&id=47 3c99f88 http://www.nr.gov.nl.ca/forestry/management/manage.stm	*Forestry Act* (1990) Provincial Sustainable Forest Management Strategy (2003) Ecosystem-based Framework for Forest Management Planning	Department of Natural Resources	Department of Natural Resources	The provincial goals are to conserve, manage, and use the ecosystems of the province while ensuring their productivity and sustainability to provide for the use of resources by the people of the province. These plans are guided by principles of sustainable development, an ecologically based management philosophy, and sound environmental practices.

Case Studies	Supporting Policies and Programs	Supporting Science Body or Programs	Enabling Organization	Description
Central Labrador (District 19A) **Area:** 2.3 million ha http://www.env.gov.nl.ca/env/Env/EA%202001/pdf%20files%202007/1351%20-%20Crown%20Dist%2019A%20Five%20Year%20Plan%20(08-12)/1351%20-%20OperatingPlanText.pdf http://www.innu.ca/forest/sec4.htm	Forest Process Agreement Forest Ecosystem Strategy Plan for Forest Management District 19 Labrador/Nitassin 2003–2023 Five Year Operating Plan for Forest Management District 19A (Goose Bay) 2003–2008	Innu Nation and Department of Natural Resources	Innu Nation and Department of Natural Resources	This co-management area between Innu Nation and provincial government aims at creating an ecosystem-based forest management plan for District 19 to protect ecological and cultural integrity, productive capacity, resiliency, and biodiversity while advancing economic opportunities for the sustainable development of forest-based industries.
Model Forest Communities of Newfoundland and Labrador **Area:** 923 000 ha http://www.modelforest.net/cmfn/en/forests/newfoundland/default.aspx http://www.wnmf.com/main/index.html	Model Forest Program (2002) Forest Communities Program (2007)	Various working groups	Western Newfoundland Model Forest Board of Directors	This model forest aims at implementing innovative sustainable forest management systems and tools; adapting their management practices and philosophies; exchanging knowledge locally, provincially, and nationally; and balancing social, economic, and ecological values.

NORTHWEST TERRITORIES

Case Studies	Supporting Policies and Programs	Supporting Science Body or Programs	Enabling Organization	Description
Mackenzie Valley **Area:** not available www.mvlwb.com	*Mackenzie Valley Resource Management Act* (1998)	Environmental Impact Review Board	Land Use Planning Boards Mackenzie Valley Land and Water Board	Integrated co-management regime for land and waters in the Mackenzie Valley.
Gwich'in Land area **Area:** 1.6 million ha http://www.gwichin.nt.ca/	*Mackenzie Valley Resource Management Act* (1998) Gwich'in Comprehensive Land Claim Agreement (1992)	Gwich'in Land Use Planning Board	Gwich'in Land Use Planning Board	This system promotes multiple uses of land, water, and resources in certain areas and controls activities in critical and sensitive environmental and heritage areas. The zoning strives to achieve a balance between conservation of the land and the use of land, water, and resources to meet human needs.
Sahtu Land Area **Area:** 28 million ha http://www.sahtulanduseplan.org/	*Mackenzie Valley Resource Management Act* (1998) Sahtu Dene and Metis Comprehensive Land Claims Agreement (1993)	Sahtu Land Use Planning Board	Sahtu Land Use Planning Board	The land-use plan will designate three categories of land in the Sahtu Settlement Area. These designations are conservation zones, special management zones, and multiple-use zones.

NOVA SCOTIA

Case Studies	Supporting Policies and Programs	Supporting Science Body or Programs	Enabling Organization	Description
Provincial Public Forest Lands http://www.gov.ns.ca/natr/forestry/strategy/code/NScodeofprac.pdf http://www.gov.ns.ca/natr/irm/	Code of Forest Practice *Forests Act* (1989) *Environmental Goals and Sustainable Prosperity Act* (2007) Integrated Resource Management Goals for Nova Scotia	Nova Scotia Department of Natural Resources	Nova Scotia Department of Natural Resources Regional Planning Teams	See Stewart and Neily (this publication).

Case Studies	Supporting Policies and Programs	Supporting Science Body or Programs	Enabling Organization	Description
Nova Forest Alliance **Area:** 458 000 ha http://www.modelforest.net/cmfn/en/forests/nova/default.aspx http://www.novaforestalliance.com/default.asp?cmPageID=77	Model Forest Program (2002) Forest Communities Program (2007)	Nova Forest Alliance Research coordination committee	Nova Forest Alliance Partnership	This model forest aims at achieving sustainable forest management through cooperative partnership within the unique context of Nova Scotia's Acadian forest ecosystems.
NUNAVUT				
Territorial Public Land http://npc.nunavut.ca/eng/index.html	Nunavut Land Claims Agreement (1993)	Nunavut Planning Commission	Nunavut Planning Commission	Nunavut land-use planning seeks a balance between development and the long-term preservation and conservation of the land, wildlife, and wildlife habitat.
ONTARIO				
Provincial Public Forest Lands **Area:** not available http://ontariosforests.mnr.gov.on.ca/ http://ontariosforests.mnr.gov.on.ca/spectrasites/internet/ontarioforests/conservingprotecting.cfm http://crownlanduseatlas.mnr.gov.on.ca/clupa.html http://www.tourism.gov.on.ca/english/tourism/rbt_management_guidelines-e.pdf http://www.mnr.gov.on.ca/mnr/forests/forestdoc/ebr/guide/natural_dist/part%20one.pdf	*Environmental Assessment Act* (1990) *Crown Forest Sustainability Act* (1994) Policy Framework for Sustainable Forests (1994) Ontario Forest Accord (1999) Ontario's Living Legacy Land Use Strategy (1999)	Ontario Ministry of Natural Resources	Ontario Ministry of Natural Resources	All forest policies and associated management practices in Ontario conform to the Policy Framework for Sustainable Forests. The framework is a guide for many activities, including forest harvesting, the management of old-growth forests, and the conservation of non-timber values. It provides the overall direction for an ecosystem-based approach to the management of Ontario's Crown forests.
Eastern Ontario Model Forest **Area:** 1.5 million ha http://www.modelforest.net/cmfn/en/forests/eastern_ontario/default.aspx http://www.eomf.on.ca/	Model Forest Program (1992) Forest Communities Program (2007)	Various committees	Eastern Ontario Model Forest Board of Directors	The Eastern Ontario Model Forest works with government, landowners, industry, First Nations, and other stakeholders to develop new ways to sustain and manage forest resources. The principle behind the Model Forest Program is to demonstrate how partners, representing a diversity of forest values, can work together to achieve sustainable forest management using innovative, region-specific approaches.
Niagara Escarpment (also a World Biosphere Reserve since 1990) **Area:** 194 343 ha http://www.escarpment.org/	*Niagara Escarpment Planning and Development Act* (1973) The Niagara Escarpment Plan (1985)	Niagara Escarpment Commission	Niagara Escarpment Commission	The plan seeks to balance protection, conservation, and sustainable development to ensure that the escarpment will be available for future generations to enjoy.

Case Studies	Supporting Policies and Programs	Supporting Science Body or Programs	Enabling Organization	Description
Oak Ridges Moraine **Area:** 190 000 ha http://www.mah.gov.on.ca/Page1707.aspx	*Oak Ridges Moraine Conservation Act* (2001) Oak Ridges Moraine Conservation Plan (2002)	Ontario Ministry of Municipal Affairs and Housing	Ontario Ministry of Municipal Affairs and Housing	This ecologically based plan provides land-use and resource management direction for a targeted area within the Moraine. The Moraine is divided into four land-use designations: Natural Core Areas (38%), Natural Linkage Areas (24%), Countryside Areas (30%), and Settlement Areas (8%).
PRINCE EDWARD ISLAND				
PEI Model Forest Network Partnership Limited (part of Nova Forest Alliance) **Area:** not available http://www.modelforest.net/cmfn/en/forests/special_project_areas/island_partnership http://www.novaforestalliance.com/default_pei.asp?cmPageID=160	Model Forest Program (2002) Forest Communities Program (2007)	Nova Forest Alliance Research coordination	Nova Forest Alliance Partnership	The PEI Model Forest Network Partnership is a Model Forest Network project operating as an extension to the Nova Forest Alliance. It encompasses all of Prince Edward Island. It consists of diverse groups working cooperatively to develop forest communities based on sound ecological, social, and economic principles.
QUEBEC				
Provincial Public Forest Lands http://www.mrnf.gouv.qc.ca/english/forest/quebec/quebec-system-management-protection.jsp http://www.commission-foret.qc.ca http://www.mrnf.gouv.qc.ca/english/publications/forest/consultation/implementation.pdf	*Forest Act* (1986) *Environment Quality Act* (2004) Forest Resource Protection and Development Objectives (2005)	Quebec Ministry of Natural Resources and Wildlife	Quebec Ministry of Natural Resources and Wildlife	Quebec is moving toward a more results-oriented ecosystem-based strategy for sustainable forest management. The Forest Resource Protection and Development Objectives (2007–2012) establish clear socioeconomic and ecological targets.
Réserve faunique des Laurentides Pilot Project **Area:** not available http://www.sfmnetwork.ca/docs/f/Carrefour%20Jette-JP.pdf	Implementation of the Coulombe Report (2004)	Scientific committee on the management of biodiversity-related issues	Partners Table (Abitibi-Bowater, local sawmills, Quebec Federation of Forestry Cooperatives, Regional Environmental Councils)	This pilot project on the implementation of ecosystem-based management focuses on the social aspects and collaborative management. It is based on a process that aims at identifying social, economic, and ecological issues.
Management Unit 085-51 Pilot Project **Area:** 1.1 million ha http://www.sfmnetwork.ca/docs/f/Carrefour%20Marchand-E.pdf	Research project of NSERC/Université du Québec en Abitibi-Témiscamingue/Université du Québec à Montréal Industrial Chair in Sustainable Forest Management (1999)	Partner universities (Université du Québec en Abitibi-Témiscamingue, Université du Québec à Montréal)	Partners Table (Tembec, Ministry of Natural Resources and Wildlife, Norbord, Regional Environmental Councils, First Nations)	This pilot project is testing the compatibility of ecosystem-based management with Forest Stewardship Council certification criteria.

Case Studies	Supporting Policies and Programs	Supporting Science Body or Programs	Enabling Organization	Description
TRIADE initiative (management unit 042-51) **Area:** 1.1 million ha http://www.projettriade.ca/		Scientific committee	Management committee (chaired by Abitibi-Bowater)	This project is based on three types of use zones: forest harvesting, ecosystem-based management, and conservation.
Forêt de l'Aigle **Area:** 14 000 ha http://www.cgfa.ca/	The Forêt Habitée Network (created by Quebec Ministry of Natural Resources in 1995)	Board of Directors (of the Corporation de gestion de la Forêt de l'Aigle)	Board of Directors (of the Corporation de gestion de la Forêt de l'Aigle)	The Corporation de gestion de la Forêt de l'Aigle (Forêt de l'Aigle management) manages the area according to the "forêt habitée" (inhabited forest) concept. It implies a multiresource management approach (forest, wildlife, recreation) embedded in a regional dynamic. The management actions must benefit the surrounding communities.
SASKATCHEWAN				
Provincial Public Forest Lands **Area:** not available http://www.environment.gov.sk.ca/Default.aspx?DN=b9517035-a2a4-4803-8d01-675215e38849 http://www.environment.gov.sk.ca/Default.aspx?DN=b2da79d5-c009-45c1-b9d9-1530b7500733 http://www.publications.gov.sk.ca/details.cfm?p=9420&cl=1	*Forest Resources Management Act* (1996) Land Use Planning Framework Caring for Natural Environments: A Biodiversity Action Plan for Saskatchewan's Future 2004–2009	Saskatchewan Environment	Saskatchewan Environment	The *Forest Resources Management Act* requires the development of an integrated forest land-use plan for management units within the provincial forest. Plans must recognize all resource values found within the forest and work with all those who have an interest in the forest to make consensus-based recommendations about how the land should be managed.
Athabasca Region **Area:** 1.5 million ha http://www.publications.gov.sk.ca/details.cfm?p=10878&cl=1	Athabasca Land Use Plan (2003) Agreement Respecting the Land and Renewable Resource Use Planning and Management in Northern Saskatchewan (1995)	Athabasca Interim Advisory Panel	Athabasca Interim Advisory Panel	The objective is to create policies that reflect the social, cultural, and economic priorities of the region, of the people of Saskatchewan, and of the advisory panel to guide future development and protection of the land and resources.
North Central Planning Area **Area:** 3.4 million ha http://www.publications.gov.sk.ca/details.cfm?p=10874	North Central Integrated Forest Land Use Plan (2006, draft)	Saskatchewan Environment	Saskatchewan Environment	The North Central IFLUP establishes three distinct land-use zones: a protected zone that calls for broad-based protection of enduring features representative of the planning area, a sensitive zone that permits resource development while recognizing and protecting a wide range of other uses, and a management zone that offers a greater scope for economic development while promoting sustainability and responsible use.

Case Studies	Supporting Policies and Programs	Supporting Science Body or Programs	Enabling Organization	Description
La Ronge Planning Area **Area:** 66 700 ha http://www.publications.gov.sk.ca/details.cfm?p=10875	La Ronge Integrated Land Use Management Plan (2003)	Saskatchewan Environment	Saskatchewan Environment	The goal is to manage the use of the land and renewable and non-renewable resources of the La Ronge planning area in an integrated and environmentally sound manner to ensure ecological, economic, and social benefits for present and future generations.
Amisk-Atik Planning Area **Area:** 4.4 million ha http://www.environment.gov.sk.ca/Default.aspx?DN=df823a51-aa64-4331-aad9-ae036016f5dc	Amisk-Atik Integrated Forest Land Use Plan (2004)	Saskatchewan Environment	Saskatchewan Environment	The plan aims at managing the use of land and renewable and non-renewable resources of the Amisk-Atik Planning Area in an integrated and environmentally sound manner to ensure ecological, economical, and social benefits for present and future generations.
Prince Albert Model Forest **Area:** 367 000 ha http://www.modelforest.net/cmfn/en/forests/prince_albert/default.aspx http://www.pamodelforest.sk.ca/	Model Forest Program (1992)	Prince Albert Model Forest Board of Directors	Prince Albert Model Forest Board of Directors	The Prince Albert Model Forest is developing new approaches to capacity building in resource-based communities and facilitating cross-sector relationships involving forestry, agriculture, and the rapidly developing mining and energy sectors of Saskatchewan.
Pasquia/Porcupine Planning Area **Area:** 2 million ha http://www.environment.gov.sk.ca/Default.aspx?DN=f359c7be-ea4e-4e62-81c4-7995bb44ccdf	Pasquia/Porcupine Integrated Forest Land Use Plan (1998)	Saskatchewan Environment	Saskatchewan Environment	The plan aims at managing the use of land and the renewable and non-renewable resources of the planning area on an integrated and environmentally sound basis to ensure ecological, economic, social, and cultural benefits for present and future generations.
Great Sand Hills Planning Area **Area:** 205 000 ha http://www.publications.gov.sk.ca/details.cfm?p=10853 http://www.publications.gov.sk.ca/deplist.cfm?d=66&c=835	Great Sand Hills Land Use Strategy (1991)	Saskatchewan Environment	Saskatchewan Environment	The strategy establishes a clear vision and goals of sustainability and ecological integrity for the area. It considers the Great Sand Hills as an integrated ecological and social system.
Saskatchewan's Native Prairie Ecosystems **Area:** not available http://www.pcap-sk.org/	Prairie Conservation Action Plan (PCAP) 2003–2008	PCAP Partnership	PCAP Partnership	The plan reflects agreement among 27 organizations regarding the conservation of Saskatchewan's remaining native prairie ecosystems. PCAP partners include representatives from industry, federal and provincial government agencies, non-governmental organizations, and Saskatchewan's two universities.

Case Studies	Supporting Policies and Programs	Supporting Science Body or Programs	Enabling Organization	Description
YUKON				
Territorial Public Land http://www.planyukon.ca/	Umbrella Final Agreement (1993)	Yukon Land Use Planning Council Regional Land Use Planning Commissions	Yukon Land Use Planning Council Regional Land Use Planning Commissions	There are eight proposed planning regions in the Yukon based, where practicable, on the traditional territories of First Nations, or groups of First Nations. The Yukon Land Use Planning Council advocates land- use planning as a comprehensive means of addressing cultural, social, economic, and environ-mental sustainability.
North Yukon Planning Area **Area:** 5.6 million ha http://nypc.planyukon.ca/	Draft North Yukon Land Use Plan (under review) Vuntut Gwitchin First Nation Final Agreement (1993)	North Yukon Planning Commission	North Yukon Planning Commission	The plan provides a sustainable development framework to balance economic development with protection of Vuntut Gwitchin culture and traditional economy, and their environment. It is based on three other principles: precaution, conservation, and adaptive management.
Teslin Tlingit Planning Area **Area:** 1.9 million ha http://www.emr.gov.yk.ca/forestry/index.html http://www.emr.gov.yk.ca/pdf/fmp_for_tttt.pdf	Teslin Tlingit Council Final Agreement (1993) Strategic Forest Management Plan for the Teslin Tlingit Traditional Territory	Teslin Regional Land Use Planning Commission	Teslin Regional Land Use Planning Commission Teslin Renewable Resource Council Teslin Tlingit Council	The purpose of the Teslin Strategic Forest Man-agement Plan (SFMP) is to provide a sustainable development strategy for the forests of the Teslin Tlingit Traditional Territory. It is a first step in defining a forest land base to which the plan would apply. This plan is intended to contri-bute to a sustainable forest-based economy, a key component of regional economic stability, while protecting and integrating ecological, traditional, resource, heritage, and other community values. It is also intended to provide a clear framework and practical guidance for forest managers and planners. The SFMP establishes the issues and concerns, values, and interests that must be dealt with as forest resource development moves forward in the region.

Case Studies	Supporting Policies and Programs	Supporting Science Body or Programs	Enabling Organization	Description
Forested Land Base within the Champagne and Aishihik Traditional Territory **Area:** 3 million ha http://www.emr.gov.yk.ca/forestry/planning_strategic.html#integrated	Champagne and Aishihik Traditional Territory Strategic Forest Management Plan (2005) Integrated Landscape Plan for the Champagne and Aishihik Traditional Territory (2006)	Research and Monitoring Technical Working Group	Champagne and Aishihik Renewable Resources Council Resource Assessment Technical Working Group	The purpose of the Integrated Landscape Plan is to achieve a forest-based economy, a key component of regional economic stability, while protecting and integrating ecological, traditional, resource, heritage, and other community values.
Peel Watershed **Area:** 6.7 million ha http://www.peel.planyukon.ca		Technical Working Group Yukon Land Use Planning Council	Peel Watershed Planning Commission	The goal of the Peel Watershed Regional Land Use Plan is to ensure wilderness characteristics, wildlife and their habitats, cultural resources, and waters are maintained over time while managing resource use. These uses include, but are not limited to, traditional use, trapping, recreation, outfitting, wilderness tourism, subsistence harvesting, and the exploration and development of non-renewable resources. Achieving this goal requires managing development at a pace and scale that maintains ecological integrity. The long-term objective is to return all lands to their natural state as development activities are completed.